RECOVERING FROM NARCISSISTIC ABUSE

How to Heal from Toxic Relationships and Emotional Abuse

PRISCILLA POSEY

Table of Contents

Preface...vii

Chapter 1: What is Narcissistic Personality Disorder? ... 1

    Types of Narcissists...7

Chapter 2: The Surprising Impact Narcissistic Abuse Has on Your Brain and Reversing the Damage 23

    The Hippocampus 24

    The Amygdala 27

    Reversing the Impact | Preventing the Spiral 31

    Hoovering 39

    The Beginning of Recovery 45

Chapter 3: Coping With Narcissistic Abuse 53

Devastation 55

Allow Yourself to Grieve 61

Reclaiming Your Power after Narcissistic Abuse 63

Common Roadblocks you may face during the
Recovery Process 67

**Chapter 4: Common Questions Asked by People
Recovering from Narcissistic Abuse 79**

Why is it Difficult to admit that I have suffered
from Narcissistic Abuse?...89

How Long Does it Take to Heal from Narcissistic
Abuse? 89

Why Can't I Stop Thinking About the Narcissist? 92

How Do I Overcome Loneliness After Narcissistic
Abuse? 94

How Do I Get Back into a Healthy Relationship
After a Narcissistic Abusive Relationship?...............98

Should I Forgive the Narcissist? 101

Chapter 5: Getting Back on Track with Trust.............. 105

How to Trust Others and Yourself Again 109

**Chapter 6: Ultimate Strategies to Overcome
Narcissistic Abuse..117**

No Contact 118

How Exercise can help you Heal from
Narcissistic Abuse 126

Acts of Kindness 129

What is EFT? 132

What are Grounding Techniques? 135

What is EMDR Therapy? 139

What are Positive Affirmations? 144

What is Aromatherapy? 148

**Chapter 7: Indications That you are Recovering
from Narcissistic Trauma and Abuse** **155**

Conclusion **163**

References **167**

PREFACE

Welcome to the beginning of *Recovering from Narcissistic Abuse: How to Heal from Toxic Relationships.* In this book, you will find out what a narcissist is but mainly focus on the ways you can heal from being involved with a narcissist. This book solely focuses on the many benefits of what you will get when you decide to start moving on from a narcissistic relationship. This book is extremely good for you to read because you will learn many techniques that maybe you haven't tried yet. It is a literal step-by-step guide on how to move on with your life. The goal or feeling you should have once you have completed this book (exercises, and reading) is that you feel fulfilled, and successful. You will feel empowered and in control for potentially the first time ever. The things you will start to experience reading this book could potentially be life-changing. If you miss out on this opportunity, you will regret it to great depths. Say you put this book down now, and you don't buy it. You will go home and be thinking about your relationship; you will go in cycles over what happened, and why. You will be stuck in a cycle of overload, and then feel the urge to call your ex. But stop, if you buy this book right now, you can finally get out of this mind trap, and learn to fix these urges, and understand why this happens.

Do you fear that you will end up in another abusive relationship? Are you the person you want to be right now? Can you honestly say that you are living the life you have wanted to live? Don't live in fear any longer; don't feel powerless to the control of others; don't allow yourself to be the victim. It is time to stand up and make real change for yourself. Because this is what matters the most. **YOU.** Your pride, your self-worth, your dignity, your mind, your body, your love, your decisions, your boundaries, your recovery. If your day-to-day is as devastating as when you ended the relationship months, weeks, or even days ago, then this book is the right pick for you. You will start to get out of this shell that you are in and dive into the mind of the narcissist and learn how to fight back. How to gain your control and be strong enough to walk away, but for good this time. Together, we can focus on loving yourself and understanding what it means to be powerful.

If you have self-esteem issues, due to the abuse, I can promise you that by the end of this book, you will be thankful for everything you learned. You will use the methods implemented in this book to help you start right now! This book will be with you every day of your life and is the smartest, perhaps the best decision you can make for yourself right this very moment. Do you want to get out of the slump of feeling so worthless? Do you wonder how long it will take to move on? Do you wish you could literally snap your fingers, and your trauma could just go away? Have you longed for the traumatic memories to disappear? Do you wish that your next relationship will be a good one? Well, this book will help you feel inspired and motivated to be better. It will teach you skills on how to let go of the trauma and find inner prosperity and peace. It will give you the peace of mind you have been searching for. Most of all, it will give you the strength to realize only you are in control.

So, if you want that control back, if you want to feel inspired, if you want to learn how to truly love yourself, and re-open your heart to others... Buy this book and love every moment of the opportunities inside. Remember, if you want to change, don't just wait for something to happen, make a choice to change for yourself. The next step is to read this book.

Good Luck!

WAIT!!!

READ THIS BEFORE GOING ANY FURTHER!

How would you like to get your next eBook **FREE** <u>and</u> get new books for **FREE** too before they are publicly released?

Join our Self Empowerment Team today and receive your next (and future) books for **FREE**! Signing up is easy and completely free!!

Check out this page for more info!

www.SelfEmpowermentTeam.com/SignUp

As A Token
of My Gratitude...

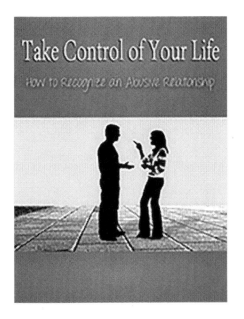

I'd like to offer you this amazing resource which my clients pay for. It is a report I written when I first began my journey.

Click on the picture above or navigate to the website below to join my exclusive email list. Upon joining, you will receive this incredible report on how to recognize an abusive relationship.

If you ask most people on the street what an abusive relationship is, chances are you'd get a description of physical abuse. And yes, that is most certainly an abusive relationship. However, abuse comes in many forms. The actual meaning of abuse is when someone exerts control over another person.

Find out more about recognizing an abusive relationship and learn how to take control over your life by clicking on the book above or by going to this link:

https://tinyurl.com/RecognizeAbusiveRelationship

CHAPTER 1

What is Narcissistic Personality Disorder?

Along with the many different personalities and traits of individuals in the world, there are also dangerous and dark personalities. One dark personality you need to look out for is narcissism. In truth, we all have narcissistic traits and may ask ourselves from time to time if we could be a narcissist; however, most of the time, we are actually trapped in a narcissistic relationship. This could be our parents, our spouse, co-workers, employers, and even our children. If you have asked yourself (especially recently) if you possess narcissistic traits or could be one, then you actually might be involved with this type of person - this is their trap to make you think you are the problem.

So, what exactly is a narcissist? It's a personality disorder (NPD), where the individual expects constant attention, becomes jealous if you don't give them what they need or want, feel superior to everyone else, and does not like or take criticism. Although, they sure like to dish it out, pointing out your flaws and everything that may be wrong with you, while they can do no wrong. They lack empathy and are the most selfish and self-centered people about. What can be confusing about narcissists or having narcissistic traits is that someone who suffers from this dark personality disorder, usually doesn't feel, think, or believe they are narcissists. This is mostly because, they don't see themselves ever doing anything wrong, and everything is someone else's fault. They hate taking responsibility, or rather, don't take responsibility for their actions because they see themselves as admirable. Although they can be charming, they show patterns of arrogant behavior, extreme need for appreciation, self-centered attitudes. They can come off as cocky, or demanding, seductive, or mysterious.

Everyone, at times in their lives, will be self-centered, demanding, charming, etc. however, if you notice it implement every aspect of their lives (with their work, family, and close relationships) you could be involved with a narcissist. So, what may cause someone to fall under the description of NPD? It is unknown like most disorders. However, some theories could be genetic, childhood nurturing, and psychological indifferences (chemical imbalances).

- Some early development risk factors include:

- "Too strict" parenting.

- Lack of sympathy throughout childhood.

- Excessive, or overpraise - spoiled rotten.

- Unpredictable schedules, with neglectful care.

- Feelings of abandonment throughout childhood.

- Constant criticism. Child feeling like they can never do anything correctly.

- Abuse

- Trauma or repeated trauma

- Development of becoming really sensitive to small things.

So, how do you know if you under the influence of this type of character? Narcissists have low self-esteem and internal problems they struggle with on a daily basis. Even though they don't show it, or may not know, they portray their attitudes and point the blame on someone else as a way to cope with their inner demons. So, narcissistic abuse is common, and also, not your fault. It's like a bully in senior high - they pick on you because they feel superior, and haven't learned how to address their problems, so they point out your flaws to make themselves feel better. Although this was a high school example, some people never grow out of this stage, and things just become uglier and worse as they get older.

Narcissistic abuse relates to any type of abuse coming from a narcissist. This can include parent-child, child-parent, and adult-to-adult relationships. Parental narcissistic abuse is when the parent expects too high or too much of their child, always asking them to give things up for their own needs, and never giving their children credit for all the good they actually do. On the other hand, Parental narcissistic abuse can be excessive praise over everything they do, not implementing enough or the right kind of discipline. This can lead to unpredictable schedules, and neglectful behavior, which then can lead to bigger problems - the child becoming a narcissist. Adult-to-adult narcissistic abuse will be discussed throughout this book, and there will be ways on how to manage and deal with a narcissist.

While a narcissist may seem tough, intellectual (for their own needs), manipulative, and sometimes scary, they are hiding something underneath the facade. NPD sufferers have problems with their confidence, and are very sensitive to criticism, leading them to be vulnerable in almost every situation they are in. It may be fair to say that the reason they become manipulative and deceiving is to cope or deal with these inner feelings of negativity. However, the things that narcissists do, say, or implement into the world is not okay and should be addressed. Although there are different types of narcissistic personalities, they all share a few things in common.

Some of these traits are as follows:

- Very self-centered. Feel more superior to others - like they are better than everyone else.

- They require excessive admiration and like to take authority above others.

- Have high expectations to be recognized or appreciated for everything they do - or don't do.

- Exaggeration of their talents and successes to make themselves look good.

- Often fantasize about the perfect relationship, success, power, intelligence, and when they fail at certain attempts to have it, they can become violent or angry.

- Manipulative behaviors to get what they want and only for their benefit

- Lack of empathy

- Belittle others they perceive as less than or not enough.

- Hold too high expectations of others.

- Unable to accept responsibility or take the blame for anything.

- Can come off as cocky, boastful, or conceited.

Symptoms or traits of the narcissist may vary depending on which kind you may be dealing with or abused by. However, in most cases, narcissists who are criticized or feel judged by others may become angry when they don't get their expected result. They can react with rage to certain circumstances due to their inability to control or manage their emotions and behaviors. Almost every narcissist has a hard time with change, or adapting to new situations, which can make them moody or depressed if anything is "out of line." It's much like a perfectionist behavior, but to extreme lengths, showing these signs in everything they do with everyone around them. A narcissist is also very good at isolating their victim - lover, children, friends, etc. for manipulation and control tactics.

Types of Narcissists

Yes, there are different types of narcissism - as every personality is different, every narcissist has their own ways to manipulate, control, and abuse you. The importance of knowing if you are dealing with narcissists can benefit you greatly to escape from their power, control, and hold over you. Almost always, when involved with a narcissist, you are being manipulated, which is abusive. Although your partner, friend, co-worker, boss, etc. may not know they are abusive, if they show any of the signs above, you are trapped in an abusive situation. So, fighting back is your only way out. The first step is to detect which narcissist you are dealing with. When you are recovering from this type of abuse, you will forever thank yourself for gaining this information as you will be able to understand and avoid falling into the same acquaintance again.

If you feel you are in a relationship with an NPD sufferer, then these signs will sound familiar to you:

- They do not give you the same attention you give them.

- It doesn't feel like a 50/50 relationship

- You feel very low, then extremely high throughout your intimate relationship.

- They can be demanding of you asking for more than you can give.

- When you don't comply, they lash out and belittle you.

- Every argument gets turned around on you as if they have done nothing wrong.

- They apologize a lot, then do it again.

- They spend your money how they want. Then get upset when you do the same.

- They take up everyone's attention over you and may publicly humiliate you.

Sound familiar? You are being abused by a narcissist. There is also narcissistic abuse in the workplace. Does one of your co-workers, or employers, bully you as if you were back in senior high. Do you dread going to work to have to deal with this person? Well, here are some telltale signs you may be abused by a narcissist in your workplace.

- They try to impress people by chatting a fair amount instead of focusing on work.

- Make promises they don't intend to keep.

- Often take credit for yours or someone else's work due to jealous feelings of you.

- They may criticize you or knock you down verbally alone, or in front of people

- May make threats while you are alone.

- They talk negatively about others behind their backs but suck up in front of them (two-faced).

- Act superior, even when they are at the bottom.

In a relationship, it is important to understand that you **cannot change your partner,** and **you cannot change enough for your partner.** No matter what you do, it's as if their behavior or problems tend to repeat themselves. So as hard as you may try to please them, and ask for things in return, the highs in your relationship are only a facade to the lows of the type of person they are.

The WEB Method

Before we dive into identifying which *type* of narcissist you are dealing with, it is important to understand the WEB method for detecting them. The WEB method consists of a three-step process; *their words, your emotions,* and *their behavior.*

Their **Words:** Their words can be an exaggerated positivity or extreme negative, derogatory words. There will be no middle ground.

Positive and Negative words: This consists of saying extreme negative things to people, or you, and exaggerated positivity to you or others. **Extremely positive** words include seductive tones or charming attitudes. Some examples of this are:

"You are amazing; I haven't met anyone like you."

"You are the best; I will make sure you get the best."

"Stay blessed because you deserve the world."

Notice how the positive words they are using are comparative. This positivity can turn **negative** quickly when you do something to upset them later on because they can quickly turn it around and use it to backtrack. Which then **can turn into** things like this:

"This person I know is really dumb, let me tell you why."

"I got rejected for my ideas at work; those people wouldn't know intelligence if it hit them in the face."

"I am going to come up with ways to get her fired; I can't wait to see the looks on people's faces when she does."

When they talk mean about people, or you, pay attention to the intent behind their words. Usually, they show signs of being thrilled about it.

Lack of empathy: As narcissists have lack of interest in sympathizing with people, they lack empathy. For example, if you explain something that really upset you, like a feeling for others, or getting rejected, they may dismiss your feelings about instantly. Instead, they will instantly reverse the conversation over to them, acting as if what you said has no effect on them, and your feelings are completely ignored.

Victimizing: Narcissists don't recognize when they have done something wrong or have emotion when they hurt you, as they take no responsibility for their words (and actions) because they feel superior. However, a narcissistic injury is when someone knocks their ego down a notch or two; when they don't feel so superior. Injuries can include being rejected, things not going as planned, or their way, and when you have dismissed them or ignored their wants or demands. This can lead them to become manipulative and strive to take power back. They become obsessed with destroying the person that hurt or "injured" them.

Your **Emotions:** Your emotions usually involve a vibe, or feeling you get when around this person. This is called your instinct and should always be listened to.

In the beginning, they may seem too great. One of the first signs is their actions and what they do. They can come off as charming, and make *you feel* on cloud nine, or extremely loved and may shower you with flattery and compliments. People who over-compliment you, or make you feel euphoric are usually never who they seem.

Before getting involved with them, make sure their charm doesn't have a different intent. Did they pick you to be their victim? Or are they just naturally charming? Get to know them before diving in.

Do you sometimes (or all the time) feel less than, when next to them? It is automatic for a narcissist to build themselves up and brag. Often times, they don't realize the impact it is having on you, especially if they steal your light, or bring you down in the process of their own success. Eventually, with this constant treatment, you may be asking yourself questions like, "am I good enough?" "Will I ever be?" What do other people think of me?" These thoughts lead to negative feelings, which then lead to more problems such as depression or anxiety.

Are you drowning? Narcissists can take the air out of the room, and leave you trying to catch your breath (metaphorically). Because their attention is solely focused on themselves and what they are going to say next, they often take up the attention in the room. They need to be center stage. You also may feel like your suffocating because they have isolated you, and diminished all your needs, as they feel like they need to come first.

***Their* Behavior:** Narcissists often make a lot of people annoyed, frustrated, or left the conversation with some sort of negative feelings. When confronted with a narcissist, pay attention to their behavior, focusing on what they do, rather than the cover-up of words and phrases they say. When you take a glance into their lives, how many friends do they have? How many people do they associate with? How do they act for strangers? Most of all, how do they treat the people (and you) that they supposedly respect? When a narcissist is confronted with their actions or words, instead of taking responsibility and reflecting on the criticism, they defend it by saying things like, "How could you, after what I have done for you."

Test this theory by telling them one of your concerns, staying away from why they would - then your concern. Then create a solution of your own and see how they act. If they fulfill your request, it's a good sign, whereas if they ignore it, and continue to do what they please without hearing you out and dismissing your concerns - take action.

Whether there be conflict or not, a small problem or an imaginative one (one they created), narcissists are always looking to point blame. If they blame you for something they have done, or for their failures, it's called projection.

For example, they may say, "I missed my phone call because you didn't remind me/ wake me up, and now it's your fault I miss out on this opportunity." So, just watch their behaviors and any red flags that come up, address them, and target your response.

Classic Narcissist

Also known as the *grandiose narcissist,* these are the people we think about when we hear the term narcissist. Everything we have learned thus far is what a classical narcissist is and what they look like. However, other narcissists share similarities but have distinct differences. A classic narcissist normally projects the blame to others while stealing the spotlight from you or someone else. They get bored rather quickly and are the biggest attention seekers among the rest. While all narcissists feel superior, the classical narcissist has the biggest ego.

It is important to note that just because you feel someone shares traits of a narcissist, doesn't mean they have the full-on disorder. According to the American Psychological Association, to be diagnosed as having a narcissistic personality disorder, you must develop instability in two out of the four psychological areas; cognitive - thoughts, effective - emotional, interpersonal - patterns of relating to others, and impulse control.

Malignant Narcissist

These types of narcissists are potentially the most damaging kind there is. Aside from having the classic traits of narcissism, they may be antisocial or inverted. They may develop a sadistic streak alongside the normal non-empathetic nature. Which means they thrive even more on torturing people and their victims. On the other hand, they also enjoy building you up to the highest point you can go, just so they can rip you down to the darkest place you imagined. Malignant narcissists are perhaps the most advanced in manipulation skills and find the experience empowering, as long as they get what they want no matter who they hurt in the process. If you are a victim or in the path of a malignant narcissist, you may feel a bunch of heartaches, emotional, and sometimes physical frustration, and mental exhaustion.

Aside from the obvious lack of empathy, a need for attention, sensitivity to criticism, charm, and egocentricity. Here are other traits a malignant narcissist develops that differs from the other types:

1. **Sadism** - A sadist is one who purposely performs pain, suffering, and humiliation onto others as a way to make themselves happy, or prideful. The distress they cause to you, makes them feel

empowered and in control, which makes them gain self-esteem and happiness. They may act like this towards people and animals or watch victimizing videos and shows to get their fulfillment.

2. **Anticipatory Manipulation** - Malignant narcissists are so good at manipulation tactics, because they implement it, and practice it on a daily basis. Most manipulators will wait for an opportunity to arise, then strike with their manipulative methods. However, a malignant narcissist will not. They proactively manipulate every day, whenever they see fit to. This manipulation tactic is the most dangerous because, if you are the victim, at first you won't realize you are being manipulated, and then eventually you will have been isolated, and torn down to a place where the perpetrator wants you to be. It happens so gradually, and by your own doing, that when you try to point the blame, the narcissist will then continue with this habit, and tell you that you are the one who made the decisions. This type of manipulation involves planning, calculating, and honing over years of practice to the narcissist.

3. **Anti-social** - Most narcissists are internally self-sabotagers, and so in this sense, it would make sense why they would develop some antisocial behaviors. They excel in lying, cheating, stealing, and have negative moods most of the time. They make for perfect con-artists, as they have a way with people from their charming attitude, and cool image.

4. **Paranoid** - Like someone who suffers from anxiety, a malignant narcissist feels like everyone is always out for their blood. Someone is always out to get them, and so they are suspicious and skeptical. With this trust boundary for others, they internally beat themselves up and show signs of confidence to gain a sense of power. They are never willing to get close enough to someone to have that someone peel back their layers, which helps them with their manipulation tactics and lack of empathy while doing it. Malignant narcissists often feel like they know what someone is doing or thinking, and so they create imaginary scenarios in their own minds, as a way to cause conflict with you. This, in turn, helps them seek control and make threats, so you don't do what their imaginary scenarios are, or so that

maybe you do, and they can catch you. Meanwhile, you are doing nothing.

5. **Envy** - Malignant narcissists hate to see others succeed and have things that they don't, so they become envious. When they see others ahead of themselves, they will purposely try to sabotage it for their own selfish needs. So, if someone got a promotion they wanted, the malignant will then manipulate the boss, or the person into why themselves would be more fitting. They may even go as far as setting the person up, to make them look bad, and then be there for when the person fails, and the boss sees them as more fitting.

With their charming traits and their egotistic attitudes, alongside their manipulation tactics with the lack of responsibility natures, malignant narcissists are definitely ones to be the most concerned about. When they feel picked on, they take two steps ahead of you to return the favor or complete their goal. Which is usually to torment, cause stress, and leave you feeling unworthy.

Vulnerable Narcissist

Also known as the covert introvert narcissist. The biggest difference from this narcissist to the others is that they stray away from the spotlight and keep to themselves most of the time. Instead, they will attach themselves to another person (a host) and use them to their advantage to get what they need. They may show signs of excessive generosity to feel the attention and admiration back. However, if they do not get the attention they want and need, they may go to great lengths to suck it out of their host, or victim.

Aside from the other narcissistic traits, here is how to spot a covert narcissist:

1. **A cocky or dominant attitude** - A covert narcissist likes to observe their audience and behave through actions or body language. When they observe other's behavior, they silently judge and come up with ways of how and when they will strike or manipulate. When you talk, they listen but don't really pay attention, rather focus on their own thoughts. Their negative behavior comes from their body language showing signs like impolite yawns, low chuckles, eye-rolls, and obvious signs of boredom

2. **Passive Aggressive** - Most introverted narcissists will insult you, but make it sound like a compliment. They will also show signs that they are listening and respond with "whatever you would like me to do," then do the opposite, or ignore it altogether. When you address them, they may make excuses like they preferred their way or accuse you of coming up with a silly solution.

3. **They often feel victimized** - When you address a covert narcissist or give them your opinions on what you think would be best for them, they don't take it as advice; rather they feel victimized. They feel as though people are not giving them positive advice, but ideas to set themselves up for disaster. With this extremely highly sensitive attitude, they will dismiss you with their smug attitudes, and plot out ways to manipulate you to get what they want instead. Later, they will say their behavior is because of you as if you made them do what they did.

When you are dealing with, abused by, or facing one of these narcissists, you need to escape from their grasp. If it is a lover or someone you love, you may tell yourself that they can change, or that if you try this, or try that, things will get better. However, when you do this, you are actually setting yourself up for failure and enabling the abuse to continue. You must set healthy boundaries, and do not fall into their traps of when things are really good, and they make you feel euphoric because no matter what, they will bring you to a very unhealthy low. Look for support, reach out to therapists, and read self-help books, like this one, to know what you must do next. Continue reading for more information on how you can escape this unhealthy relationship and recover after you get away.

CHAPTER 2

The Surprising Impact Narcissistic Abuse Has on Your Brain and Reversing the Damage

Narcissistic abuse is one of the most damaging abuses out there because it affects you emotionally, and mentally. It can come in forms of physical, verbal, and mental abuse, so the quicker you catch the signs, and the faster you identify the narcissist, the better off you will be. Believe it or not, this kind of psychological abuse leads to the physical changing of the brain, according to recent studies. Because narcissists don't feel empathetic toward anyone's feelings, they don't see the consequences they cause or the damage they implement. It is proven that with long-term narcissistic abuse, part of your brain actually shrinks, and changes its shape. This leads to cognitive problems and mood disorders such as anxiety, depression, and even bipolar.

The two parts of the brain that change their form or shape with continuous narcissistic abuse, are the hippocampus, and the amygdala. The hippocampus is the region of the brain which focuses on memory and learning. The amygdala is the region of the brain that is responsible for forming and development of negative thoughts and emotions such as guilt, shame, fear, and envy. Over time, with constant abuse, comes the physical shrinking of the hippocampus, and swelling of the amygdala.

The Hippocampus

The hippocampus is part of the limbic system in the brain. The limbic system focuses mainly on processing and developing feelings and responding with actions or reactions. The limbic system also included the amygdala and the hypothalamus. The hypothalamus works together with the amygdala and creates the nervous system and the endocrine system. These systems regulate, balance, and control body functions. So, if the hippocampus is damaged, or the amygdala becomes disrupted, you may experience more suicidal thoughts, panic attacks, and flashbacks, or nightmares. This is out of your control when you have experienced such abuse for long periods of time. However, you can fix this by escaping your present nightmare and managing ways of dealing with stress and preventing yourself from enabling this type of relationship again.

Short-term memory is the first step to learning; without it, we wouldn't learn anything. The hippocampus stores these short-term memories, then later converts it into long-term memory or "permanent" memory. Stanford University and the University of New Orleans implemented a study, which found that there are strong links between high levels of cortisol (a stress hormone) and damaged or altered hippocampus. This means that the more damaged the hippocampus is (shrinking, swelling, etc.), the higher the possibility of high cortisol levels will surge through the nervous system. When we have high surges of cortisol pumping through us, we may feel things like dizziness, experience panic attacks, become moody, overthink, worry, fret, etc. Basically, the more stress you have, the smaller your hippocampus is, which is not a good thing.

Hippocampus is the core of our memories. We have two types of memories, which includes the declarative memories, and the spatial memories.

- **Declarative memories** relate to facts and events. An example would be learning the lines to a play, the lyrics to a song.

- **Spatial relationship memories** are more in-depth memories that involve pathways and routes. Some may say the spatial memory is our photographic memory. So, an example of this type would be that you memorized how to get from point A in a city you don't know to point B.

As talked about before, the hippocampus converts our short-term memories into long-term ones, then finds a different place in the brain for these long-term memories to be stored. What is interesting about the hippocampus, is that it is always generating new nerve cells, and continues to develop on a daily basis. So, it makes sense why long-term abuse would frustrate, or damage the development and shrink.

The shrinking of the hippocampus has been linked to long-term stress, or abuse, which then leads to trauma, which involves PTSD signs, and sometimes schizophrenia. Since evidence shows in recent studies that stress is one of the main causes for the shrinkage of the hippocampus, it makes sense why escaping narcissistic abuse is beneficial to start lowering stress and reversing the cortisol levels; you may experience when under this amount of pressure.

The Amygdala

The amygdala is mainly responsible for controlling our instinctual, core emotions, and functions. These include lust, fear, hate, love, along with heart rate, body temperature, breathing, and sugar levels, and blood pressures. When the amygdala is on high alert, it implements physical symptoms to the rest of the body, which is where the "fight or flight" response comes in. The fight or flight response is a response the body reacts to sending symptoms like trembling, sweating, feverish, dizziness, etc.

These symptoms can be alarming, but most of the time, they are "false alarms." Narcissists keep their victims on high amygdala alert, making it difficult for their victims to manage stress. So, when the hippocampus shrinks, it produces excess cortisol levels, and then the amygdala becomes triggered, it also sends out the same response that cortisol will apply. With this in mind, the hippocampus has now stored short-term memories into long-term memories, which are triggered by the abuse resulting in PTSD. When the amygdala is swollen as a result of the narcissistic abuse, anything can trigger this "fight or flight" response. So, you are stuck in a downward spiral of panic, and fear over the smallest things, which can be smells, sights, and even feelings. This is because what we see and experience, our brains are trying to relate to what has happened from before - pulling from our memories - and if those memories are traumatic, it triggers the amygdala to apply uncomfortable, disabling symptoms.

In short, the amygdala is the reason we are afraid of things or the reason we love things. It controls how we react or perceive the world around us. Based on our experiences through life, the amygdala is our control for how we respond to events that cause our emotions. If the amygdala is swollen, we will most likely react to everything - or small things - with fear and see them as a threat.

So, say you managed to escape the wrath of a narcissist. If you were in the relationship (parent, spouse, employer, etc....) for a long period of time, you would have developed PTSD, heightened fear, phobias, panic attacks, or depression. This is because the stress that the narcissist caused, caused your amygdala to swell, which then the amygdala has gotten used to living with heightened awareness, and seeing everything as threatening. While in the relationship, the victim (you, for example) will use coping mechanisms such as bending reality defense strategies. These are as follows:

- **Projection:** You may convince yourself that your abuser has goodness in them and that if you try harder, be better, or "bow" to them more, they will treat you better, but you are just struggling right now. With narcissists, this is rarely the case, and all you are doing is making excuses to stay in the relationship longer.

- **Compartmentalization:** You may only be focusing on the positive side of the relationship, completely ignoring the abuse and the negative, thus still defending your abuser. By doing this, you are telling yourself that this type of behavior is okay, thus training your brain that this way of heightened fear and the way you are living is normal. Hence the lasting effects of the narcissist.

- **Denial:** Because you feel it is easier to live with the abuse, rather than confront it, or escape from it, you may make excuses for yourself like, it's not as bad as it seems or as it feels.

The process where your brain has to create new neural pathways comes strictly from the hippocampus. Everything we do, learn, know, read, and understand is all the responsibilities that the hippocampus takes care of. With a shrunken hippocampus, it becomes harder to focus, takes longer to understand and learn, and we have to put more effort into doing things that were easy to us before. We may lose interest in things that we loved, partially because we don't have the drive, motivation, or energy to do it. This can all happen from narcissistic abuse.

The hippocampus shrinks due to the increased hormone surges of cortisol (the stress hormone response). The cortisol then stimulates the amygdala or triggers it, which is the cause for our thoughts to become fretful and anxious. So, it is essential to learn stress-reducing techniques to prevent this from spiraling - even if you aren't associated with a narcissist.

Reversing the Impact | Preventing the Spiral

As with most disorders, chemical imbalances, and therapeutic methods, there is usually a cure or a "way out." Of course, it takes drive and dedication, but when you want something bad enough, you will be able to get it. Techniques like Eye Movement Desensitization and Reprocessing therapy (EMDR) is good for learning how to cope or overcome PTSD or trauma symptoms. EMDR calms the amygdala, which allows room for your brain to react and respond to situations more rationally and logically.

Other methods include aromatherapy with essential oils, meditation and mindfulness, acts of altruism, and Emotional Freedom Technique (EFT). EMDR and EFT are explained in more detail in chapter six of this book. Before you can start practicing these techniques and coping methods, you first need to escape the narcissistic abuse.

Why You Feel You Can't Leave a Narcissist

Abuse is everywhere, and more often than not, implemented in most relationships. Sometimes we do it to our spouse, colleagues, friends, or children, and we may not even notice. Other times, we are the ones being abused. However, narcissistic abuse is the most damaging to our psychological state. Oftentimes, people have a hard time leaving an abusive relationship because leaving would be changing, and change is a scary thing for most people.

Here are the most common reasons people don't leave abusive relationships, narcissistic or not.

1. **Our society acts as if it is normal, so an abusive relationship is hard to understand or accept** - Since there are so many people going through abuse, our society, plus the media, creates abuse as something normal. As a relationship starts, it's normal to feel the euphoric highs, and the lows don't start until later on. But when the abuse starts to happen, we often don't realize until it's too late, and when we do notice, we fear the change of leaving and don't accept the situation we are in.

2. **Self-esteem becomes less than before, so starting fresh becomes even scarier than normal.** - Long-term emotional, and psychological abuse, like narcissistic abuse, changes our thinking patterns making it difficult to build self-confidence. Because you aren't physically abused, you may not feel as though the

abuse you are going through is even as bad. However, mental abuse, in most cases, is actually worse than or equal to physical abuse. Once you have in your head that you are worthless, you may actually feel you deserve this life and find it easier to stick around rather than leave.

3. **Abusive cycles happen; after every abusive incident or fight, a make-up phase follows.** - After a real low, the abuser will then apologize, or do things to make up for their crappy behavior. This leads us to believe that there is hope and that your relationship can last. So, you tell yourself that because they are sorry, they don't deserve to be left behind. Then you come up with more excuses for them, which results in sticking it out longer. Then the abuse happens again, and so the real lows, are followed by the high highs again, repeating this process.

4. **Sometimes it is dangerous to leave, and the victim may be more afraid to leave than stay.** - Especially in physically abusive relationships, men or women are more likely to be killed after a break-up has happened, over the time of the relationship. A malignant narcissist has the same

thought pattern as a killer, so the victim may be terrified to leave, so they stay for their safety.

5. **Society expects people to survive "no matter what" when in a relationship** - The pressure of having a "perfect" relationship means that we stay no matter what. We may feel judged or looked down upon if we leave our spouse. Loyalty is shown to be of the utmost importance with the "ride or die" attitudes in society.

6. **"Gaslit" behavior from our abuser keeps us in the relationship longer.** - Gaslighting means that the abuser will turn the blame or a situation around on you, and make you think something is your fault when it actually isn't. With, this being done constantly, the victim (you), may feel the need to stay as if their behavior is somehow your responsibility.

7. **"Things will change."** - How many times have you said this to yourself, or maybe your friends? We have this perceived notion that things were good once upon a time, and so with the right attitude, and both of you trying, things can get back to that. Maybe you think your partner is only

acting like this because things are hard, or stressful, and with the right actions, and you taking on more responsibilities, things can go back to normal. The fact of the matter is, these are excuses, and we make excuses because we are scared to leave. An abuser's behavior won't change, because let's face it life is stressful, and there will always be problems. It is not up to you or anyone else to change your partner or change for your partner in hopes of things getting better.

8. **You share your lives together** - So, this is maybe the number one reason people stay. They feel familiar, and a sense of security with their spouse. Maybe they got married, had children, bought a house, shared expenses, and this is all they know. A life without this person by their side would look or potentially feel even more miserable than they already are, so they stay. The truth of this belief is that even though you share your life with this person, you don't have to finish your life with them. Abuse makes people codependent, and so the victim doesn't feel confident to leave and live a life of their own. In these cases, it is best to get a lawyer, or therapist's advice, to help you make the change.

When you are under the control of a narcissist, they are master manipulators. This means that they isolate you, make you feel weak and vulnerable, then convince you that they are all you need by building you up and setting others up to make you think twice about your friends. Then when you fight or have arguments, you can never win, and never escape because you are isolated, and they control you. Your mind no longer becomes as happy and fulfilled as it once was, your drive becomes unmotivated, and your life seems to fit only with their schedule.

To fight back, we often make five horrible mistakes.

- **Blaming yourself -** Because of the belief that we are to blame, (narcissists doing), we put the blame on ourselves which drives us to try harder, do more, and push ourselves past what we are capable of. However, the battle never seems to end, so we are abusing ourselves by enabling their behavior and letting it affect us. Meanwhile, they are sitting there laughing on the inside.

- **Making threats -** To gain some self-esteem or some sort of power back, we may look or search for their weaknesses and exploit them, causing us to have to make threats. However, threats only work if they are followed through, when you don't follow through, you lose your power. On the other hand, if you do follow through, you may feel even more lost than you did before for having to stoop that low, so you apologize, and the cycle starts again.

- **Trying to be understood -** Have you sat there trying to interpret messages, or body language, or words and sentences your spouse or narcissist has spun? You are making your best effort to relate to them, come up with solutions, and give them what they need, but want them to do the same. So, in your efforts of trying to understand them, you make the mistake of getting them to understand you. You may try repeating yourself, showing them what you mean, or even rephrasing what you are trying to say. However, they continue to return the attention back on themselves to make their own point. The true fact here is that they do understand you. They know what you mean, or what you are talking about. However, they only care that they are heard, they don't care about coming up with solutions for you, as there is no compromise with them. They simply just care about themselves.

- **Withdrawal -** After a long night, days, or maybe even weeks of fighting with them, you finally just give in. You become numb to feelings, and your own emotions and your energy has run out. So, you give up. While this helps with saving your energy and mental exhaustion, it does not get you out of the situation you are in.

- **Denial -** When we are confronted by our friends and people who love us about our relationship, we make excuses, or lie to hide the abuse. By doing this, you are only letting the narcissist win, because as long as you continue to make excuses for them, you show them that their abuse is secretive, which only gives them more power over you.

The truth is, is that you will never be able to deal with a narcissist. When you try something, they will always turn it around on you, When you give into them, they will somehow make you feel like your efforts are unnoticed, or that you are still at fault. Basically, no matter what you try to do, you will always be in the wrong in their eyes, and they never will be. The best method on dealing with a narcissist is to escape their wrath, and become independent, by learning personal growth strategies to get where you want and need to be. You must learn to live without them.

Hoovering

Here is a perfect example of what hoovering is: you and your ex have been over for a while. You haven't heard from them, and they haven't heard from you. You are finally getting on track to where you need to be; you may be going to school and making new friends. Maybe you are finally eating healthy and patched a broken friendship from before. Your life is finally heading in the direction you want. You will always remember the love and care for your ex, and you are finally moving on. All is right in the world. But then, out of the blue, you get a text or a call from your ex. It says, "I need you, I am in a dark place, and I just want to die. Please help me." Your heart speeds up, you swallow your throat, and butterflies flutter in your stomach. Against your better judgment, you answer with "what do you need?" Flashbacks of the abuse and your relationship come to your mind, along with all the good times that happened in your relationship.

This is hoovering. The minute you answer to them, you have fallen right back into their trap. Hoovering is a manipulative tactic that a narcissist will use to draw you back in. Think of hoovering as "sucking" you back in.

Hoovering is done when some time has passed, and the narcissist will target their victim's weaknesses or vulnerabilities to get back what they had or want. When you give in to this manipulative tactic, they have won, and you fall back into the cycle you tried to escape from.

Narcissists hoover because they need to regain control. For whatever reason they have to draw you back in, most times, it's because you are an easy target. From being an easy target, they know they can get sex, validation, attention, affection, money, and even power. Perhaps the most defined reason they hoover is because they feel empty. Narcissists, as mentioned, need to feel wanted, or superior. When they aren't getting this attention, they hoover you, to get what they want as a way to fill that void inside them.

Narcissists are hungry for attention, to the point of it becoming their first and last thought of every day. When they don't get or have attention, and they can't seem to find it with anyone else, they will pick on their exes to have it back - meaning you become their victim again. They pick on their exes because they already know things about them, and most of the time, their exes are easy "prey." Because they know you; or, they think that they do, and they will exploit your weaknesses and have you coming to them. This continues, until they get bored of you, or find something better, then leave you, in which case you have fallen back into the abusive cycle again. The problem as to why you get hoovered is because you care too much, or have too much empathy for them, not realizing that they don't have or share the same feelings. They don't care, they just want what they want, and when they don't have it, they destroy to get it.

Types of Hoovering

There are many types of hoovering. However, some of these forms of hoovering may be done currently by the person you recently ended things with. One objective of hoovering is that is almost always done by a narcissist, with no other intent than to suck you back in, so that they can take advantage of you all over again. If an ex is doing this or has done these following hoovering techniques, it's best to ask yourself one thing. Is my ex a narcissist? If they were not, and things were just up and down, then your ex is not hoovering you, they are only trying to win you back after all this time. On the other hand, if your answer is yes, pay close attention to the following kinds of hoovering. When reading them, think of it like the way your ex is thinking, not yourself.

1. **Pretending or acting as if nothing happened.** - Narcissists will pretend as if everything is okay like nothing has happened, and that you are still in a relationship. They will ignore your requests to cut ties and may show up at your house, work, or even your family members house to reach you. They will send happy faces in a text and leave complimentary messages on your voicemail. This is one hoovering technique.

2. **Sending gifts** - Attempting to win you over again, they will go out of their way to send you things. This may include your favorite flowers, chocolates, gift cards, movie tickets, concert tickets, and even money.

3. **Apologizing** - They will apologize for everything they have done. They may even write a letter explaining in great detail about how "sorry" they are. As convincing as they are, there is only one thing you need to do. Think back to the beginning of your relationship - the honeymoon stage. If they are saying or doing the same things they did to win you over in the first place, it's fake.

4. **Indirect manipulation** - If you have managed to ignore all their attempts thus far, they may think outside the box and contact people you know, such as friends and family that are close to you. They will either tell your close relations lies so that the message will get back to you, so you feel the need to correct them, or talk to them, and at this very point you have been hooked, and reeled in. Or, they will start to send really happy positive things to your family, in an attempt to show them they are trying, and have your family say that you should talk to them for closure reasons. Don't do this. The most effective, or manipulative message for if you have children with the narcissist, is that they will get your children to lure you back home.

5. **Declaring love** - Since love is such a strong emotion, they may send you love letters, write you poems, or explain in great detail all the good of what they remember what had happened. They will express their deepest feelings in the most romantic way. This is a powerful hoovering technique and should be ignored at all costs.

6. **Sending "out of the blue" messages** - You may see random texts saying things like,

> "Please wish *John* a happy birthday for me."

> "Are you going to that social event we talked about? It's tonight."

> "I am at the place we went to on our third date. I remember what you were wearing, and how romantic it was, do you?"

7. **Faking the need for help** - This is perhaps one of the nastiest tricks they can pull, and usually do it when they feel absolutely desperate. You may get a text or voicemail saying that they are going to kill themselves because they are at an all-time low. They may make up some fake illness like cancer, or heart issues so that you will come back to them out of feeling obligated or guilty. This technique preys on the natural instinct most people have for compassion.

Note that hoovering is a narcissists way to "suck" you back into the abusive relationship. They will do whatever it takes to remind you that what you had was good. Because most of us are empathetic and like to reason or try to our best efforts, they know this and prey on these instincts. Hoovering is lying techniques, manipulative methods, and disguises to get you to come back. With this in mind, you can ignore the behavior, and get a restraining or protection order of some sort so that you never have to deal with it again.

The Beginning of Recovery

Recovering from any type of abuse is hard, but escaping, and recovering from narcissistic abuse takes patience and dedication. You will have to continuously remind yourself of all the benefits, and the setbacks. Relapses will happen, and it may take a few tries to leave. once you have finally escaped their wrath, it is about commitment to yourself for a better life. I will explain briefly about the six stages for recovering from narcissistic abuse, which are as follows:

Stage One: Devastation

This stage is the first stage in moving on. You may feel emptiness, shock, depression, find it difficult to concentrate, or hold conversations, anger, and some bitterness. At first, you may feel number, and disappointed, maybe a little confused, and your mind will be flooded with the positive sides of your relationship.

Memories of you laughing or going on dates may make you want to turn back, but it is crucial to understand that a narcissist will not change if they don't want to. It is also unfair to ask anyone to change themselves, and so this part of the process is needed.

If you detach yourself or withdraw from the world, this is okay. Give yourself time to release all this energy and feel the feelings that arise during this stage. It may feel like working becomes a hard task, eating becomes difficult, or binge eating becomes a habit. This happens because you will feel numb, lost, and like you have lost all control. The confusion comes from the loss of your relationship, wondering why it couldn't work, remembering the many things you did or didn't do. This is the first stage of moving on, while you experience signs of withdrawal, it's like a drug that you need to get away from. This step is normal, however, if it lost for a long period of time, seeking professional help may be in your best interest.

Sometimes, in this stage, you may be holding onto guilt or shame. This is because the narcissist still has a hold on you. They have manipulated your mind and twisted your words so many times, that even after they are gone, there is a part of you that believes you deserve this pain. Don't let their grasp keep you thinking you are nothing, worthless, or even crazy. You are not, and as long as you feel and think this way, they have won. The best revenge is showing them that you can survive without them.

Stage Two: Allowing yourself to grieve and be angry

So, after finding out that you are a victim of narcissistic abuse, you may feel that the relationship was one-sided and that you should not allow yourself to feel angry or grieve the relationship. This is false. Absolutely let yourself grieve. Let yourself be angry, and miss the relationship, just don't allow yourself to go back, or give into their hoover efforts. If you don't let yourself be angry and grieve, then you could actually be setting yourself up to fall into another abusive relationship down the road. Here are other things that could potentially happen if you don't allow yourself to be angry and grieve:

- Staying stuck in the devastation process longer than you should.

- Anger builds up. Temper problems.

- Trust issues.

- Unnecessary exhaustion, and depression, or stress for prolonged periods.

- Addiction.

- Avoidance patterns and habits.

- Chronic pain or illness.

- Obesity or eating disorders.

Once you have felt the anger, and carried the grief, allow yourself to move forward. Although, this may take some time, remember to continue to beat this one day at a time, Some days will feel harder than others, and other days will seem easy. The next step is to take care of yourself, no matter what.

Stage Three: Taking care of yourself

As we have learned, emotional, stress, or any type of stress can damage the brain. So, as you are grieving, and going through the waves of depressive states, to anger, bitterness, and finally acceptance, you need to make sure to take care of yourself. Read self-help books, and positive quotes every day to start feeling better and growing in your personal life. Surround yourself with positive and supportive people. When you are ready, get out and meet new people again. The emotions you feel is your mind and body's way of processing the stress and complexity of the situation. So, learning how to regulate your physical response to your emotional reactions is key to becoming healthy again. Some things you can do to take care of yourself are as follows:

- **Meditate and practice mindfulness whenever you can**. It is proven that when you meditate or become aware of the present moment, you can reverse the symptoms from the abuse you experienced. Go somewhere quiet, take in ten deep breaths (breathing with your stomach), and calming your mind by enforcing positive thoughts, and mantras.

- **Exercise every day.** This is crucial because when we exercise, like going for a run, take a nature walk, do some light yoga, etc. we don't focus on the breakup, anymore, but rather focus more on what we are doing. Exercise releases endorphins, which are feel-good hormones that our minds need to feel good about ourselves. The goal is to let go of the emotional energy by learning to love exercise and getting rid of the negative baggage in a healthy way.

- **Get enough sleep.** It's bad enough that the emotions that have you spiraling down are keeping you exhausted. Ensuring that you get enough rest is one of the fastest ways your body can recover from withdrawals and the emotional heartache you feel. If you cannot sleep, listen to guided meditation exercises, and let follow all the steps until you feel calm. Remember, there is always tomorrow that you can think of all the things your mind is telling you right now.

- **Eat healthy.** taking care of yourself means that you take care of your body as well. Nine times out of ten, the reason why people develop such mood disorders is because they don't eat right. Healing your gut heals your mind, which develops good chemicals, and helps balance your emotions.

Stage Four: Objective analysis phase

This phase happens when you have pushed past the devastation, felt the anger, and now all that seems like a distant friend or foe. This is where you need to be thankful for everything that has happened because it has shaped you into the strong person you now are. You can finally look back, without the attached feelings post-breakup. This is the stage where you are ready to get out of the slump you were in and help others who are suffering, or who have suffered the same as you. At this stage, you may find yourself having old feelings come slipping through the cracks. And this is normal, but the feelings won't seem so overwhelming or uncontrollable as you have tried hard to rebuild yourself so that the emotions don't have such a strong hold of you anymore. This will be a good feeling.

Stage Five: Acceptance and reintegration phase

Acceptance is about seeing things for the way they are instead of having a clouded vision or the "wool pulled over your eyes." The narcissist no longer has a hold on you, and you have accepted that what was can never be again. You understand your worth, and you know what to look for, and what not to fall into. At this point, you know all the signs, and realize that the grasp of the narcissist was unhealthy, and so if another unhealthy relationship starts to happen, you will be able to take action. Trust your instincts.

Stage Six: Ensure that you never become abused again

The last stage of your recovery is to make sure that you never have to go through something like that again. Oftentimes, people that have not healed fully from an abusive partner, or from the trauma, will accidentally or automatically fall right into another abusive situation. Researching and finding out the main areas or concepts of narcissism is not the answer to ensuring you don't fall into their trap again. The main reason for falling back into an unhealthy relationship is because we have not developed personal growth, or have fully healed from the last one, and so when our gut instincts scream at us "no," we ignore it, and just do it anyway because it's all we know.

Because all narcissists are not the same, the second narcissistic relationship you fall into will implement some other tricks, and without the previous wound is completely healed, you could fall into their trap again and result in having another terrible traumatic relationship .It's best to heal the wound completely so that this pattern doesn't continue.

So, do the inner work needed to heal your heart, educate your mind, and take good care of yourself through every step. Be cautious but not too cautious because you could miss out on great opportunities. Focus on getting rid of the garbage, and heal your mind, body, and spirit to release this negative energy and spot signs of narcissism early on. Continue reading for in-depth strategies on how to overcome and rid yourself of narcissistic abuse.

CHAPTER 3

Coping With Narcissistic Abuse

If you have ever been in a relationship with, or are experiencing narcissistic abuse, then you probably know how hard it is to leave. You know what you need to do, you think about the ways you can escape, and you gain the courage to do it, but then, you don't. You don't because something brings you back in. You sit there and think of all the good memories, then think about what would happen after you actually left, then you think about all the things that haven't happened yet, or maybe if you stayed things would get better due to whatever excuse you come up with. This is another form of fear. Your mind has you trapped as a result of the abuse to the point where, when you do decide to or try to leave, you feel a flood of panic. The fear is something many of us can't seem to overcome, so we stay in the relationship hoping that things will get better, or that things will be okay. But it never does, so you start from the beginning, getting ready to leave again. It's a vicious cycle that no one should have to go through. If you find yourself sitting there most of the time asking yourself, "should I stay, should I go," then you most likely already know the answer to this, and should go. Things don't get better; they only repeat themselves. The narcissist you are involved with will always make promises they can't keep, and they will always build you up for the main purpose of thrashing you down.

In the previous chapter, we talked about the stages one will go through once they finally leave for good. As much as the first stage is painful and hard, I hope you see why it's needed for the final stage to happen successfully. Devastation is difficult to manage, but with the right support, you will get through and finish all the stages, and be at a point where you view your ex as a person you knew but has no hold over you. I promise you that if you reclaim your power after getting through the dark side of your breakup, you will come to a realization that without sacrifices, you will stay stuck. No one likes to be stuck, and no one needs to feel the way you do right now. So, get up, release yourself, and become one with who you are by starting the first stage of the breakup.

Devastation

So, we have already talked about devastation, but did we talk about ways to get through it the easiest way possible? No. When we are devastated, we don't want to do anything, eat anything, speak to anyone, and we would rather drown our sorrows under cozy blankets, and cry into our pillows. The devastation comes in a few different stages and can come all at once, or one by one. First (or last) comes the shock that you are actually done, that your relationship is actually over. Memories will pool inside your mind and flush you back to what was. Next, you may feel numb, or cry (a lot), with the feeling of not caring about anything. Your eyes may hurt, you may not be able to sleep, which makes you unable to concentrate on anything, and you could withdraw from the rest of the world because you would rather do this alone then have anyone see you as pathetic as you feel. Next, anger will set in. You may become bitter to people around you and forget to take care of your needs like clean the house or get dressed. Anger will consume you if you let it, but this is part of the process of healing. To get past this feeling, you feel like a "rebound," will help you get out of this slump. So, you put on a fake smile, get dressed up, and go out on the town to get under someone else, so that you feel the affection you crave so much. This is called denial. You are in denial about your feelings. You think you are ready, but you are not. If you do this, you most likely end up with the same type of person you were just with, thus resulting in more damage to yourself later down the road.

As much as devastation hurts, and you may want to do everything to stop feeling that aching pain in your chest. Have the flashbacks go away every time you hear a song, turn the TV on, or go out; you can't. The best way to get through this stage is to learn techniques that will help you deal with these overwhelming emotions. It is important to remember that although this stage is needed for a successful final stage if you let yourself feel this way for too long, you will never recover. So, instead of remembering your lowest point, reminiscing about the good and bad memories, remembering all your fights, and all your efforts, or trying to come with answers to why you were so badly treated, stop. If you continue to do this, the pain only escalates and keeps you in the devastation stage longer than you need to be there.

Instead, try these tactics to help you speed up the process of devastation:

1. Closure

The stage of devastation may be so hard for some people that they often go back to their spouse in this stage. After all the crying, and the anger, maybe a couple of rebounds, and they decide to go back. This is not healthy, because next time you leave, you will have to start this process all over again, and I don't need to remind you what happens to our brains when we are under this type of stress. So, just end it. If you have made the decision to leave, then do that. Get your closure, write letters (send them or don't), say your goodbyes (physically or to yourself), and do whatever you need to gain some sort of closure. Then, don't go back.

2. Externalize

This stage is the mindful stage - in which we will talk more in detail about later. However, it revolves around knowing and understanding how you feel and being patient with these feelings. It's about accepting the hurt that you feel, but not clinging to it. Knowing that there will be better days, and right now, it is okay to let it all out.

3. Appropriate process

This is a necessary process to help you cope with the devastation because it allows you to make sure you are not obsessing over the breakup and your feelings. It comes in five steps:

a. Admit the pain, or anger

b. Vent, and let it out to the people who are most supportive - or write about it.

c. Determine your response to your emotions (are you going to sit here and feel sorry for yourself, or are you going to try to get up and take care of yourself today?)

d. Stick to your goals, and your plan to recovering and making it through this first stage of devastation

e. Forget it. Shift your thoughts to something else, something more positive. You can only learn to forget once the other steps are taken care of.

4. Distraction

Devastation will destroy your sense of accomplishment and hold you from doing things you used to enjoy. This stage in the process is to fight back - do the opposite of what you feel. So, if you feel like sitting in bed all day, get up and sit on the couch, or outside for the day. Distract your mind with telephone calls to loved ones, play crosswords, exercise, write, draw, etc. Do something creative, and don't allow yourself to sit with this pain.

5. Maintain your schedule

Whatever your routine was before, continue with it. If it is hard to fully maintain a routine right now, just do a couple a day, then gradually increase your strength to move on to the next thing you used to do. For example, if you used to wake up and go for a run, come home shower, get ready for work, go to work, come home and make dinner, then read a book. Start by just getting up and going for a light walk and having a brisk shower. Day by day, increase your routine to one more thing on that list.

6. Find a place that doesn't trigger you.

If your breakup consisted of them moving, and you are stuck with all the memories no matter where you look, consider moving or staying with a friend for a while. If you had to move, and it hurts to go out and see the places you guys walked or went on dates, avoid these places, and find somewhere new to go. Just don't avoid it forever.

7. Give in to the need for closeness - without sexual contact

The fastest way to get through this stage is physical closeness. So, if you have a child, cuddle them, if you have a best friend, ask for lots of hugs. When you need a shoulder to cry on, reach out to someone you trust. Along with this physical closeness, bonding with people you trust is a bonus in this recovery.

8. Avoid all things sexual

Although physical closeness is essential for recovering from a narcissist breakup, sexual entanglement with someone can make things worse. If you haven't completely moved, on you may feel shame, guilt, and even more anger. We want to avoid this as much as possible.

Devastation is the first stage of recovery, and it may also be the hardest. However, when you make it through this stage, you can move on to start taking better care of yourself, which will make you feel good. In short, you must let your feelings sink in, don't fight them, take care of your well-being, and stay off the internet or forums (at least for now). The last thing you want to do is overwhelm yourself with research that reminds you of your narcissistic relationship.

Allow Yourself to Grieve

Believe it or not, crying, and tears are beneficial to your recovery. Crying is scientifically proven to rid your body of stress. When you let your other emotions in, this also helps with the grieving process. However, if you hold your emotions in, you are making connections in your brain that suggests holding it in is a better solution and will actually cause more problems for you later. When people hold their tears, and anger in, they never learn to release or let go. Instead they teach themselves that it is okay to hold it in, which can result in an outburst later. Have you ever cried so hard, then after you get this foggy feeling, but it feels as though a weight has almost lifted? This is because you have relieved yourself of the tension or stress that you feel.

Tears are our body's way of releasing stress, fear, grief, anxiety, and frustration. Tears can come in many forms or feelings like tears of joy when a child is born, or tears of relief when something has ended for the better. For some people, they don't cry or release the tension in this way because they feel weak or pathetic when they do. Crying, and shedding a few tears is not by any means a sign of weakness, they are signs of strength and authenticity. Tears have more than one purpose other than just relieving stress. They contain antibodies that fight pathogenic microbes and remove irritants. There are three types of tears; reflex, emotional, and continuous.

- **Reflex;** These types of tears well up in our eyes to remove irritants like smoke, or exhaust fumes.

- **Continuous:** This tear contains a chemical called "lysozyme," and are there always to keep our eyes lubricated to avoid them drying out. Lysozyme protects our eyes form from getting infections.

- **Emotional:** Emotional tears are the ones we release for stress and anger, as already explained. They happen when we are sad, angry, stressed, or overwhelmed, etc.

Tears travel through the tear duct and into our noses to keep that section bacteria free. Ever noticed after crying, you may be able to breathe better, and your heart rate decreases? That's because of the emotional stress we released; we enter a calm or emotional state. It could also be because crying can be exhausting, but it does make you feel better. Dr. William Frey at the Ramsey Medical Center - an expert on tears - says that emotional tears have a buildup of stress hormones in them. So, when we cry, we release them, which, in an additional study, says that by releasing the stress through our tears, it gets replaced with an endorphin - the happy hormone.

Reclaiming Your Power after Narcissistic Abuse

Think back to what you went through, from the ages of 0-12. During this stage in our lives, we are constantly learning and growing into ourselves. To understand today, you need to first understand what happened in those years of childhood. For example, if you were abused, neglected, abandoned, lived in foster care, etc. through the learning stages of your life, you may feel like you need affection or become codependent now. Narcissists can pick this type of vulnerable person out of a crowd and give them what they need so that the narcissist benefits. So, it's time to ask yourself about you. What about you? Narcissists will make you feel as what you need, and what you want doesn't matter. They set or hold high expectations of you, tell you to shut up, sit down, and just do your job which is to give in to their needs. They make you feel as what you say and do doesn't matter, which then causes or is the result of codependency. So, when someone tries to tell you what to do, or dismiss your thoughts and feelings, reevaluate the situation and out loud or internally say, "what about me?"

This is why it is so important to figure out the "template" of what you have been brought up by. For example, if you have been ignored, or seen as invisible through the ages of 0-12, then you probably sought attention, and have been bred into letting go of your own needs for those around you. Which are what codependents do, they drop the needs of themselves to please and constantly put the needs of others in front of themselves for the hope that they will be seen for their efforts.

When you try to leave a narcissist, they may try throwing in your face "how could you," or "if you loved me you would do … or wouldn't do …" It is up to you to fight back with creating boundaries and looking out for number one - which is you. If your spouse or loved one doesn't see that you have needs as well, then they are either a narcissist or are not looking out for your best interests. You need to be able to confidently and assertively say "if you loved me, you wouldn't demand these things of me," or "you would instead ask how I felt, or if I can or even wanted to." By reclaiming power this way, you set boundaries, and are also teaching yourself that you are important too. Learning to respect ourselves by setting boundaries, and not giving into the narcissist's tricks gives us our power back. It also teaches the other person boundaries, and which you are putting your foot down about. In the future, when you sit down and ask yourself and your spouse, "what about me?" it will show you are also thinking of your own needs. If your relationship respects you, they will take a minute and understand that, or they won't. This doesn't necessarily mean that you don't have to do what was requested of you, but first, before making sacrifices, you must make sure that whomever you are associating with you thinks about your needs, wants, and feelings attached to the request as well.

Shifting Into Your True Powerful Self

The one thing most people don't realize is that everyone has lower self-esteem that whatever happens to us externally, triggers our internal defectiveness. What I mean by this, is that we all have that powerless self, we all have those thoughts that we may not be good enough. It's the narcissist's expertise to pick these powerless, and uncontrollable "flaws" about us and exploit them. They intentionally find our weaknesses, and blow them up, then convince us that they can help us and fix those qualities. For a while it works, then without them, you feel powerless again, and eventually, you feel powerless all the time because even with them, they make you feel as you couldn't make it without them. You are simply powerless.

To take back your power, you need to understand your true self. Your true self consists of feeling no pain, but rather, acceptance, joy, and wholeness. It is the non-judgmental part of you that exists without reaching out to other people to take our pain away. When we give the power to someone else to help us find and heal ourselves, we fall back into the same codependent trap, and never truly feel one with ourselves. The key to reclaiming your power is to overcome each stage of moving forward and dropping the person you were when you were with the narcissist. Let go of the victimized soul that you used to be, and strive for happiness, and confidence that you are stronger than this. If we can't do this, then we give into the powerlessness from what the abuser made us feel. Now to get through this, we need to figure out what is haunting us the most on the inside and tackle it. If we feel empty or abandoned, we look for ways to overcome these feelings in the most healthy and positive way we can. We never stop working on ourselves, and we never give the power to someone else to fix us and what is inside. Otherwise, the patterns that we implement throughout our lives will never change.

And this is the final step to reclaiming your power, is to be true to yourself and be honest with whom you are. Take control and tackle the "defective" qualities within.

Common Roadblocks you may face during the Recovery Process

Escaping narcissistic abuse is not easy; in fact, it may be one of the toughest things you can break free of. With their control, extremely impressive manipulative ways, and hoovering techniques, you may find yourself going back to them more than you want or staying in the relationship longer than you should. This chapter heading was designed so that you avoid making the common mistakes most make when trying to recover or move one. By following the next steps, you will stop wasting time, and be able to recover quicker.

1. **Believing that researching more about narcissists will make you better** - This belief stops you from moving forward because it triggers the abuse that you just went through, thus stopping your process from succeeding. This is because the rational and logical analyzing part of your brain has no direct access or contact with the emotional part of your brain - I like to call it the wise mind, vs. the emotional mind. For example, Say you got shot in the leg, then you

research about guns, shooting, leg wounds, etc. Researching about it doesn't stop it from happening, and it doesn't take away the pain, or the damage already done. So, the more we focus on our trauma, the more work we are going to have to take to get to the next step, which is healing from the trauma, rather than focusing on it.

2. **Assigning blame** - Blame is what you do when you feel someone is right, or when someone is wrong. The problem with blame is that we are blaming our narcissistic relationship for what they did to us. This childish notion stems back to when we were in our learning concepts of youth and giving the power to someone else to give us what we feel to be anger, sadness, joy, or other emotions. Instead, we shall not blame (even ourselves), but just accept that most of our actions were a cause from ourselves. We got into the relationship, and we stayed longer than we should have. We are in charge of our decisions, and whether or not we made the right or wrong choices, we learned from them. The main reason we blame others for providing or not providing for us what we need is because we haven't yet learned to provide it for ourselves, which gives us codependency and the

habits of being with people that seek out our weaknesses for exploitation purposes.

3. **Staying busy to distract ourselves from the pain** - If we cannot heal ourselves and face the pain head on, and deal with it, then how can we expect anyone else to love us. Distracting ourselves away from the trauma the narcissist caused only implements more hurt down the road, and we never truly heal. It's like if we ignore our car breaking down, or a leak in our roof, and pretend it's not there. just to find out when we come back to it, the damage is still there. If we don't want to live with the pain or damage that the leak has caused, then we will fix it, or otherwise, confront the problem. This goes in the same way as us. If we are damaged and don't manage the feelings or cope with our trauma, when we sit alone by ourselves, the trauma, pain, and damage are still there, as we have not dealt with it yet, thus getting triggered again.

4. **Replacing the love of another with the love of someone else** - Most people would call this a "rebound," in which case it is. We want the love and attention of someone else, because we were so badly hurt by our narcissistic spouse or loved one. One of the problems that could happen with this type of

behavior is that when you try to replace your narcissist partner, you may come up short, which then makes you crave the attention of the narcissist even more. Another problem is by doing this, you could actually damage your brain, or emotions even more, which could result in permanent self-esteem issues or at least more codependent tendencies. We cannot let someone else love us or give us affection if we don't put forth that example for ourselves. What is most attractive to a non-narcissistic person is a person who can care for themselves and provide their needs both physically and mentally.

5. **Keeping tabs on the narcissist** - One of the most destructive things we can do in our recovery is to figure out what the narcissist is up to. It only keeps their hold on you and makes you want them more. The trick is to completely let go of your life with them by providing no contact to get better and thrive on your own. Questions like "do they still love me, miss me, care for me, think about me," are pointless because instead of focusing on ourselves, we are putting the focus back onto them, and our trauma. One thing about narcissists is certain. They don't care, they never did, they used you for their own benefit, and they would do it again if they had the chance. If we

don't feel like we are good enough to be loved, we will constantly seek validation and reassurance of our worth from another. We need to learn the worthiness of ourselves, by practicing self-healing before moving onto another person, and that is the key to reclaiming our power as well.

In short, the things we want to do, like check up on the narcissist, replace their love, assign blame, become distracted from the pain, and constantly researching about narcissists is contradicting to our healing process. As long as we don't do those things, and focus solely on love for ourselves, positivity in our minds, and taking care of ourselves, we can put the narcissistic abuse aside, and finally, grow into who we know we can be.

A few bonus roadblocks to your recovery process is as follows.

1. **Not admitting to yourself that the narcissist is dangerous to your emotional and physical well-being.** - This stems back to the "wise mind" vs.. "emotional mind." Our emotional mind is obsessed with coming up with excuses or reasons why it is impossible to leave. Why you should stay, and why it will work out if you did this, tried this, etc. We get

trapped in the notion that the narcissist can change, or that they will want to. That maybe they aren't a narcissist, and the highs and lows you are going through are normal. However, if you feel like you constantly need to prove yourself to your partner, or if you tried harder, or whatever excuse you want to become real, then you are living with a narcissist. Healthy relationships don't ask you to prove your worth. Instead, they accept you for who you are and move in the same line, same path, and same expectations together. If you see yourself as a victim, you will always be one. On the other hand, if you see yourself as successful, you will be. It's called "Law of Attraction."

2. **Unrealistic expectations of the amount of time needed to recover** - Because of the feelings that we want to be loved, held, and noticed, we often try to rush the recovery and healing stages. Just when we start to feel better, we may think that it's all done, and then jump into something else faster than we should. When we expect the process to take a certain amount of time, we set ourselves up for failure. However, when we just let things be, and continue to work on ourselves and let whatever happens come naturally,

we forget about the expectations of how long, and eventually we are just "better."

3. **Avoiding the hard work to move forward** - the trick in moving on, is you have to be ready to. You have to *want* to. If you are not ready and don't want to, then you are forcing yourself into the recovery process without putting your full heart or effort into. Sometimes, people stay in the relationship because this is what they know. It feels good to get the sympathy and attention from others that they aren't getting from their loved one, and almost feel as though that would end too. But this is why it is important to give to yourself what you expect or want or are getting from others. Since moving on, and changing your life is so hard, you may become fearful of the whole process, and stay where things are easy. But look at it this way; are things actually easier if you stay? or could you put in as much effort as you are into this relationship as you could in yourself? In fact, being true to yourself, and letting yourself heal and go through the process of loving yourself takes a lot less stress than staying with a narcissistic partner. If you are not ready to walk away just yet, know that there will come a day where enough will be enough, and from there, you can finally face the future to move

forward with no fear, because enough will be just that. Enough.

Throughout the recovery process, and with more information you are about to read, make sure to remind yourself that you deserve happiness. Remind yourself that you are the only one in control of where your life leads you. Be a good example for the people around you and be the positive self-caring image for yourself and what you need. If you are still unsure about what you should do next, the next chapter should answer all your questions about your relationship and yourself.

WAIT!!!

READ THIS BEFORE GOING ANY FURTHER!

How would you like to get your next eBook **FREE** <u>and</u> get new books for **FREE** too before they are publicly released?

Join our Self Empowerment Team today and receive your next (and future) books for **FREE**! Signing up is easy and completely free!!

Check out this page for more info!

www.SelfEmpowermentTeam.com/SignUp

Just a Friendly Reminder...

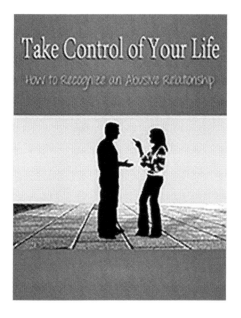

I'd like to offer you this amazing resource which my clients pay for. It is a report I written when I first began my journey.

Click on the picture above or navigate to the website below to join my exclusive email list. Upon joining, you will receive this incredible report on how to recognize an abusive relationship.

If you ask most people on the street what an abusive relationship is, chances are you'd get a description of physical abuse. And yes, that is most certainly an abusive relationship. However, abuse comes in many forms. The actual meaning of abuse is when someone exerts control over another person.

Find out more about recognizing an abusive relationship and learn how to take control over your life by clicking on the book above or by going to this link:

http://tinyurl.com/RecognizeAbusiveRelationship

CHAPTER 4

Common Questions Asked by People Recovering from Narcissistic Abuse

W hen we dive into something new, we are often fearful of the changes that lie ahead. Our emotional mind attacks us with questions and can often keep us awake at night pondering about all the things our future holds. We may fight with ourselves about whether or not to go back, tell ourselves lies or beliefs that things could be different, and even defend our betrayal against others. The truth is, is that we cannot get along with everyone, and so when we get involved with someone, and fall for them, it is natural to have arguments, disagreements, and lows. Every relationship goes through these things, whether you are intertwined with a narcissist or not. However, the dangerous signs of a relationship are when our arguments become ultimatums, our disagreements become fearful fights, and the lows outweigh the highs. Relationships are difficult as it is, and normally when you care about someone and love someone, it is natural to want to keep your relationship together and fight for everything so that the years are not lost. But, like the last chapter says, "what about me?" If your relationship feels one-sided, and with all your efforts, the other person has to **want** to change and **want** to walk the same path by your side as well. Narcissists don't think about your feelings, and they don't **want to**. That is the key factor when addressing your thoughts and asking yourself questions that you need to be aware of.

No matter which type of narcissistic relationship you have experienced, or may be currently in right now, you are most likely questioning the same things most in your position are. The common questions every narcissism victim has asked themselves are as follows:

1. **How do I get the narcissist to change?** - The thing about change is that when we try to change someone else, we are actually "accidentally" trying to control them. The truth here is that you can **never** change someone. You can only change your own actions and responses to their behavior. The thing that most people forget to do over time with their spouse, friend, coworker, etc. is that they forget to accept the person for who they are. If you cannot accept them for who they are, then you may want to try techniques to change them. Nonetheless, this is the wrong approach. If you can't accept how they are now, then you need to ask yourself if you can deal with this person how they are now without anything changing for a lifetime. If your answer happens to be no, then you are the only one in control of your next action to this response.

2. **How can I keep my children from being abused or hurt by a narcissist?** - Have you ever heard of *"monkey see monkey do?"* Children spend most of their time learning how to act, what to say, or who to be from their influences. If your co-parent's actions and behavior revolve around narcissistic ways - manipulation, lying, lack of empathy, neglect, etc. then you may be dealing with alienation syndrome. Most narcissistic parents will use their narcissistic

ways to influence children to reject the other parent. Most of these strategies that the narcissist will use are brainwashing techniques, which can do serious damage to your parent-child relationship.

So, if you are the parent on the other end of the narcissist, and it is impossible to limit the other parent's influence on your child, then follow these next suggestions;

- Teach your child critical thinking knowledge

- Role model a positive and safe environment for your child - avoiding becoming controlling, neglectful, and fearful experiences.

- Spend quality time with your children to get to know them on a deeper level. Build and grow your bond.

- Relax. Enjoy your life with your kids, without living in fear of what the narcissistic parent is doing behind your back.

- Be an adult. Meaning, do not put yourself in the same position as your children or give power to your co-parent.

- Seek support from a professional, like a therapist, or counselor. Go through family therapy to figure the best option for what you can do in your situation.

3. **How do I respond to a text message or a call from the narcissist?** - As hard as this answer may be for some of you to accept, the best approach is to cut off all contact. This may make you scared or fearful of what they will do if you ignore them. It may make you in your head about what game they want to play next, or how they are going to plot against you. However, by responding to them, you are giving them what they want - attention. It is best to block them from everything, text, calls, social media, etc. If you bump into them in public, avoid contact with them as well.

   If they are a co-parent, family member, boss, or someone of the sort where you have to keep in contact, keep the conversation on point. Keep it short, and sweet, simple and straightforward. The goal here is to not let the narcissist hoover you back to them or manipulate you more. If you are new to this process, ask a third party to help you with the messages, as they won't be involved, and will be able to tell the difference between manipulation and straight forward talks.

4. **How do I manage "silent treatment?"** - The silent treatment is another way of a narcissist to hoover you or manipulate you. If you understand this and recognize the signs or the intent behind the silent treatment of your abuser, then you **must** avoid this behavior. Do not respond or associate contact with them. The silent treatment is a hurtful control tactic from the narcissist to get under your skin. When you ignore it and don't let it bother you, you are gaining some of your control back. Which will show them that this will not be tolerated. If you cannot get away from this person, distract yourself with something else. It is important to note not to take things personally and remember that the silent treatment is just another form of abuse. It is not about something you did or didn't do, and it's not something you deserve or earned.

5. **How do I co-parent with a narcissist?** - It can be extremely difficult to co-parent with a narcissist or someone who has traits of the sort. The best approach to answer this question is to set up some sort of legal documents on the time that is spent, and how parenting will work. That way, when it comes down to

it, you won't have to contact this person as much, and it will be legalized so there are fewer fights about it. Another route is to set up family counselors or attend parenting classes together.

6. **How do I break free from a narcissist relationship?**
- The reason it may feel impossible to get away from the narcissist is not only to do with love, but you have developed a "trauma bond." As "Good Therapy" explains, and I quote[1] *"The "addiction" to the person with narcissism is really an addiction to the brain chemistry attached to the anticipation and traumatic bonding within the relationship."* What this means is that narcissists are addictive because of the constant up-down cycle they put you through. When we are abused, or brought down very low by our abuser, the only way to get through the low, is when our abuser brings us up again. This creates the "trauma bond," which becomes addictive, and can be a difficult process to escape from due to some withdrawal effects.

---

[1] https://www.goodtherapy.org/blog/common-questions-asked-by-people-healing-from-narcissistic-abuse-0507184

To work through this, you must follow the stages and take care of yourself. It will be hard at first, and it always gets hard before it gets easier. This is where friends, family, therapists, and other supports can be a real benefit to you. You may feel like you want to withdraw from the world, or only talk to the narcissist themselves, however, fighting these feelings is the only way to break free.

7. **How do I heal from growing up with a narcissist?** - This takes time and practice, and it basically stems down to getting to know yourself internally. Children that are raised by narcissistic parents have learned to use their parent as a guide of how to act, speak, and behave. Look inside yourself for the answers, A few steps to try are these:

   a. Find your voice.

   b. Learn if you have dissociated or developed other "serves" to manage and cope with your childhood

   c. Be kind to yourself. Be inspirational and positive for yourself.

d. Create positive affirmations to tell yourself every day - "I am enough," "I am not responsible for anyone else's feelings."

e. Surround yourself with positive and 'safe' people.

f. Talk to a counselor, or psychologist.

g. Join support groups.

8. **How do I recover from estrangement with my child?** - Perhaps the most painful thing that can happen to a parent is estrangement from their children. Your emotional mind is going to want to kick in and explain to your child the truth, in hopes that they would turn to you again. However, by doing this, you are stopping to the narcissist level to get your child to turn on them, which will only make your child confused, and matters worse. So, you may be stuck with grief, sadness, despair, and hopelessness. Seek guidance from a counselor in which they can help you with the following:

a. Reminding you that it's not your fault.

b. Live life to the fullest of your ability.

c. Keep communication lines open.

d. Learning assertiveness and boundaries.

e. Not allowing yourself to be abused by your children.

f. Listen to your child non-judgmentally, even if their truth isn't the truth. Listen with kindness and empathy while not tolerating disrespect.

g. Practice self-care and self-kindness.

h. Offer your help or love to others or paying it forward.

i. Do not give up hope. Tomorrow is always a new day, and it's best to live each moment with an open and ready heart.

As hard as narcissistic personalities may be to handle or manage, you need to be stronger than the abuse they make you feel. You can only do that by learning and growing for yourself every day. Every day is a new opportunity to do something new, face your fears, and challenge yourself to grow.

Why is it Difficult to admit that I have suffered from Narcissistic Abuse?

Denial is the first part to any breakup. It's also the main reason why it can seem so difficult to admit to the narcissistic abuse you just went through. Regardless of if you are still in a relationship with them or not, the attachment is still there, and the games that they play are still taking control of you. If you have caught yourself thinking 'they will come back,' or 'one day they will wake up and realize what they did was wrong.' You are in the denial stage. Even though you have foregone the abuse, it's like without them, you are still holding onto the idea of you being together again. As long as you hold onto this thought, they still gain and have power over you. Denial minimizes the truth of what is right now. Meaning, what is happening right now is that you and your spouse have now become ex's, or the relationship is over and has been for a while. You just haven't come to the realization of accepting this yet, because anything past this point is scary and new.

How Long Does it Take to Heal from Narcissistic Abuse?

How long it takes is not the question, but what do I need to do to heal? - is a better one. Pain is the barrier which causes *how long* the healing will take. So, when you focus on healing the pain, is when you can start understanding how long it will take to heal from the abuse. If we sit there and pretend that the pain does not exist, or we distract ourselves from the pain by being with someone else, or diving into work, the healing process will take forever - literally. It can feel like you are taking two steps forward, and then three steps back, to be put in the exact place you were trying to avoid in the first place. This happens when you don't deal with the emotional pain that the narcissist has caused.

Anxiety, depression, and other mood disorders like PTSD all stem from trauma and pain that we haven't dealt with. It's our body's way of telling us that the pain is not going anywhere and give us the opportunity to take the trauma and turn it into lessons that we can grow from. The process in dealing with our pain and trauma or abuse is to feel it, hold it, and then release it in healthy ways by taking care of ourselves. Eventually, we will learn that through these dark times in our lives, and how we manage to get through them is who we truly are on the inside. Our experiences shape us to who we are going to become, and everything that has happened to us up to this point shaped us to who we are today.

Talking and venting about our pain to other people is not going to fix the pain or heal our problems; it will give us a short release, and a quick endorphin rush. However, you may find that when you are alone, the pain just gets worse, and this is because we aren't dealing with it ourselves. We lie to ourselves and convince our souls that we are fine, that it's just a little problem, and that we don't need to put the work in to get where we need to be because we aren't actually that bad. This is not the case, and it's a lie we tell ourselves to avoid the pain and hard work that we need to put in.

There are three things you can do to deal with your pain:

- Going towards the pain and feelings associated with the pain

- Completely feeling the pain, and the emotions

- Opening our heart with love and non-judgment to it

The pain does not go away if we distract ourselves or tell ourselves that we are okay. The truth is we need to accept that we are not okay, we need to understand that we are upset, and we need to be patient with ourselves for the time it takes to tackle each emotion that comes forth.

When we have thoughts of diminishing ourselves, bullying or beating ourselves up for what could have been done, or what should have done, we are only making the pain worse, and the healing process will take longer than it needs to. In short, treat yourself for how you would treat someone you loved unconditionally who would be going through this, like your children. What would you say to your best friend if they told themselves what you were to yourself? As though this may not feel like it would work for you, write two letters. One letter from yourself, to yourself, then the response as if you were righting back to a friend. Everything you say in the response letter you need to actually implement through the process of dealing with your pain.

Why Can't I Stop Thinking About the Narcissist?

So, we have researched, read about, talked to, and tried our best to get over or through our narcissistic abuse or trauma. We have finally reached inner peace, and may even start to feel a bit better, however, the answer to this question - why can I not stop thinking about my abuser? Is this; you are addicted to love. You are addicted to how you felt when you were with the narcissist. The way a narcissist "loves" us, is them finding out our weaknesses, exploiting them, and giving us validation in a way that we never experienced before. We get this behavior confused with 'love' because it's a good and addictive feeling. But one thing is for certain. Narcissists don't feel love. They may think about or implement love in other ways, but mostly they just 'love' you because they are getting what they want from you by manipulating you into believing you are getting what you want.

And, we are attracted to or pulled in by the narcissist so easily because what we experienced love was as children, or in our early development years, is all we know, and all we know what to look for. If our childhoods were traumatic, and we failed to get the attention we needed, then we crave it all the time. When the narcissist gets a grasp of us, they feed into our desires and show us a different way or world about what love is. And this could be different for everyone.

When we are children, we model after our parents, and so if they treat each other wrong, or judgmentally, then we will observe with judgment and treat people wrong as well. If our parents are too lenient on us, then we learn to use people or whine to get our way, and never grow up past this point. Then we will go through life behaving as if we are superior; this is how a narcissist is born. Also, if our parents are too strict, then we may feel as though we aren't good enough, and everything we do becomes dismissed, which then we want to continuously please people. We look for love in others that our parents could not give to us because we have not been taught how to love and take care of ourselves; this is how a codependent is born.

So, the reason for why you can't stop thinking about the narcissist is because they either gave you the love you never had, or the attention you crave, or the feeling you missed with anyone else. Or, you are stuck wanting to please people and be respectful, or good, or enough for someone and the narcissist made you feel as though you weren't good enough. They were an example of what you had lived within your early development years, which would make sense for why you question yourself now. This is because you haven't learned how to properly take care of yourself and love yourself unconditionally for who you are today.

How Do I Overcome Loneliness After Narcissistic Abuse?

As most things do, loneliness also stems from childhood, early development years. As children loneliness can stem from neglect, or abandonment from our parents, or caretakers. Then unconsciously, unaware when we become adults, we fall into abusive relationships because they cover up the 'wound' that we have buried inside us - loneliness. Then we are afraid to leave, for the feeling that with almost every abusive relationship we have been in, they have isolated us, and took us away from our friends and family, in which case they become all we have. So, when they are gone, we are back to feeling lonely again, which may be a feeling we feel impossible to overcome.

When we are left to be alone, with maybe one or two people by our side, this often does not become enough. So, we will actively look for companionship, or someone to be around so that we can escape this loneliness. This cycle is essential for our growth to be able to break it. The answer to the question is to embrace the loneliness and to let it in. Just like pain. We need to learn how to deal with the discomfort of loneliness. You can be alone without feeling lonely, or you can be around a bunch of people and feel like the loneliest one there. You have to be willing to be alone so that you don't fall into the cycle of getting into abusive relationships in the future. Because, when you are alone, you get to be with yourself, and get to understand yourself on a deeper level, which is when you can do the most healing.

However, being alone is not the same thing as being lonely. Being alone is when you are not with other people, you are not surrounded by anyone else. Being lonely is an emotional state. So, you can also be alone without feeling lonely, and this is the goal we need to achieve. It is also best to stop complaining that you are always alone. Do not seek attention on social media, or vent to people all the time about how you are so lonely. The last thing you would want is to have a narcissist nearby, and then target you, which then you fall into another abusive relationship time and time again.

There are two cures to loneliness:

- **Presence:** Meaning to be completely here with the here and now. Being completely mindful of what you are doing right down to the literal sense. What are your toes doing? what color is the room you're in? If you are eating, what does it taste like? Be completely in the present moment. It's not overthinking, worrying, or obsessing over things you cannot control, but being completely one with this moment right now. When you find yourself distracted or focusing on something else, bring yourself back by asking, "where am I?"

- **Authenticity:** Meaning being 100% you and who you are. Standing up for what you believe in, and just being completely authentic to who you are, and escalating the vibe externally. It does not please others, becoming the person that someone else expects you to be, doing what others want you to do, holding inside what you want to say, etc. You need to feel completely free and comfortable to be who you are. The question to bring yourself to being authentic is "who am I?" Think of three adjectives that describe you for your ideal self.

The last little bit that you can do to break through the feelings of loneliness is to take time for yourself. This is truly beneficial when you put time aside to look after you. It is not selfish, but, instead, it is responsibly selfish to understand your importance and needs. You need to look out for yourself, otherwise, how can you focus on work, college, relationships, parenting, etc. If you are looking for others to take care of you. At the end of the day, you should be the only one that is there for you. When everyone else leaves, and things don't go as planned. It is only when you take care of yourself that you find true internal happiness.

If this hasn't helped so far, the next best thing is to find companionship in an animal. A dog or a pet can be beneficial for many reasons and will never betray you. Animals are great healing mechanisms you can enjoy. I suggest a dog, because you can train them, bond with them, go for walks with them, talk to them, and they will only show you loyalty and respect back.

How Do I Get Back into a Healthy Relationship After a Narcissistic Abusive Relationship?

The answer to this question is dynamic, because when you are in a relationship with a narcissist, they attack your confidence, your power, self-esteem, and isolate you to feel worthless. If you haven't done the work to fix what the narcissist broke, then you won't have a healthy relationship, because you will be looking for in your next partner what they took from you, which can result in getting involved with another narcissist or abusive partner.

To get involved with another relationship that is healthy, you first must address the CPTSD - Complex Post Traumatic Stress Disorder. CPTSD happens when you repeat the process of an abusive relationship, such as being with a narcissist which can make you think or have triggered emotional flashbacks. CPTSD can be stemmed from childhood trauma when you are emotionally neglected, (or any other form of abuse), and if you haven't been in a childhood traumatic situation, the narcissist can make you suffer from this as well. It is a type of disorder that is an ongoing trauma that implements intrusive, unpleasant, and repetitive memories that fire off like alarms. In short, your brain literally screams at you to "look at this," "think about this," "then this happened," "you need to think about it first." CPTSD also implements overwhelming, and unwanted emotions that seem to come out of the blue, because your brain has made connections subconsciously to the triggers that you may be facing from the past trauma you experienced.

Another thing that can happen from being in a narcissistic relationship is that your 'super-ego' gets hijacked. In short, your super-ego controls your ego. So, it tells your ego how to act, what is right, what is wrong, and so forth. If you have been the victim of emotional trauma or abuse, your super-ego will become inflamed and damaged, which then your rights become wrongs and vice versa. It will send you negative messages about who you are, and also send you emotional flashbacks that you can no longer control. Which results in CPTSD.

So, the question here is, what do we do if we want to get into a loving relationship that is healthy for us? We have to reduce the emotional flashbacks, and if we don't do this, then we will constantly be triggered by our past, in which we will put the blame onto our new partner, which will cloud our vision of who they truly are. Also, when you are vulnerable or stay in this CPTSD state, the more likely you will fall into another narcissistic relationship again. Because what they will do is spot these weaknesses, and put you where they want you to be, to stay stuck in this mind state. The next thing you must focus on is healing your super-ego. If we haven't healed the inner critic part of us, then you will also likely fall back into a similar relationship. This is because your intrusive thoughts will tell you that you deserve this, and when you believe that you actually deserve the abuse, you are settling for less than what you can have - a healthy, loving partnership. If you don't work on the superego part of your brain, then your perception of love will always feel as though belittling, gaslighting, not being good enough, trying unnaturally hard, is love. It is not.

You basically want to get to a state where you can easily process, feel, and own your own emotions, so learn about emotional intelligence as quickly as possible. When you learn emotional intelligence, you will easily be able to pick out an abuser aside from a lover, as you will know and pick up on the cues and be more in tune with your own personal instincts.

Three things you must do, and when you search for support through therapy, you can achieve these goals for gaining a healthy relationship. Heal the inner critic - super-ego, take care of your CPTSD, and finally learn emotional intelligence.

Should I Forgive the Narcissist?

Most of us say to ourselves, or others that we want to forgive our abuser, but somehow, we just can't. The answer to if you ever will honestly doesn't matter. Whether you do, or you don't, it's entirely up to you and makes no difference if you did or not. The reasons why forgiveness is not always the answer are as follows.

1. **You need to move on.** - Just like the hoovering techniques, a narcissist will use, focusing on whether or not you should forgive is actually one of them. The reason for this is, once you forgive them, you are more likely to go back to them, as they will convince you that if you can forgive them, things will change, and it's needed for the relationship to grow. However, narcissists have a disorder. Disorders do not just

'change.' It takes realization, and then a few stages to go through before accepting that the disorder is here, which takes years of work. If you follow them through these years of personal growth, you will only be hoovered back in to get abused more until that happens IF that happens.

2. **It's time to focus on you** - When you ponder the thought about forgiveness or not, you are avoiding, or procrastinating self-care. Self-care is one of the most beneficial and quickest healing processes you can do to move on. When we learn how to love ourselves, it becomes quite difficult for a narcissist to break through. This is because narcissists have no love for themselves, and do not understand someone having the power that they need or crave for themselves. So, they would rather pick on a different victim.

3. **Forgive yourself instead** - The main forgiveness you need to focus on is forgiving yourself. Forgive yourself for putting yourself through the abuse for longer than you should have. Forgive yourself for not being able to take care of who you are. Forgive yourself for being a lesser version of yourself. Finally, forgive yourself for the lack of effort you gave yourself for growing and being 'powerful' again. Use

this opportunity to make up for the things you forgive yourself for.

4. **You need to heal** - Everything that has been said prior to this chapter is everything that you need to do for yourself to heal. Feel every emotion that comes with devastation, feel, and grow with your alter egos, or super-ego. Tackle the CPTSD trauma you implemented. Take care of yourself and fight back on those negative self-images. The faster you heal, the better off you will be. Sitting there focusing on forgiving your abuser, may or may not make you feel better, but you have far more things to work on than forgiving someone else. It is time to put yourself first.

In short, the forgiveness of the narcissist is entirely up to you. If it makes you feel better, go for it, if it doesn't serve you, then don't. However, in order for success, and the answer to most of your questions come from within. When you ask questions about the relationship or trauma, or abuse, or the future, or people you care about, whatever it may be. Know that you have the answers already, and just need to look inside yourself to find them.

CHAPTER 5

Getting Back on Track with Trust

Living with a narcissist or implementing a real relationship with a darker personality disorder person can leave you second guessing everything. This is because you no longer trust yourself or others around you and is why it is so crucial to heal through personal growth, to get past this. The biggest reasons why trust seems so difficult after a narcissistic relationship is because you are fearful that it will happen again, being alone has now become very new, and new things can be scary, and the narcissist has damaged your perception of life, and so you see everyone as a narcissist. If trust already doesn't come easy to you, then learning to trust again, may be even more difficult.

Depression, anxiety, and CPTSD are common side effects when you go through narcissistic or emotional abuse. Some tactics of an abuser include negative criticism, control, verbal threats or punishment, belittling, gaslighting, mind games, lack of trust or loyalty, isolation, and ignoring. The consequences for staying in these types of relationships can put an emotional strain on the body and the mind where the victim is left to believe they are unable to be on their own or 'survive' without their narcissistic spouse.

Luckily there are things we can do to get better, gain our trust back, let go of fear, and accept change. The following are just a few suggestions to get started.

1. **Take your time** - Time is power, and power is what a narcissist will try to take from you. It is completely normal to feel even more threatened or afraid once you leave the relationship. This is because during your relationship, your abusive partner 'allowed' you to go when they told you, you may have constantly been questioned or controlled, what you believed in wasn't

good enough, and they became unsupportive of your beliefs. Now that you have escaped the relationship, you may constantly be looking over your shoulder, or checking your phone, in case they are in the dark depths of every corner of your life like they used to be.

The truth about taking your time is that the abuser may have made you feel lost, confused, alone, and questioning what you should do and where you should go. You may be used to being told what to do, so you search for the acceptance of others before you do something. Your life is yours to live, not theirs, and regardless if you are in a relationship or not, it's only your choice on what you do, how you do it, who you spend your time one, and where your path is leading you. These are all things the narcissist makes you question about, and if you have stayed longer than you should when it's over, you may be untrustworthy of the what, where, who, when, and how. Self-care and healing take time after a relationship like that, and you need to take your time with it. Don't question the process, or how long it will take until you trust again, just start healing, and trust will come naturally to you as gradually as it is going to take. Accepting this is your first step.

2. **Create boundaries or revisit them** - Boundaries teach yourself and others how to respect you. Through boundaries, you can start healthy relationships, promote confidence, and become accountable, or hold others accountable for actions. The thing you need to understand is that your needs matter and the only person who is going to make your needs happen is yourself. Again, it is your life, and only your choice who you want in it, and how you want to spend your life with those people in it.

3. **Be knowledgeable** - It is not the best solution to start researching and learning all you can about abuse and narcissism right away after your breakup. However, when you are ready (when you start to feel better), start learning about what you went through, not as a way for revenge or selfish purposes, but as a guide in what to look out for. When you do research, focus not so much on the abuse, but more on how to love and take care of yourself, look for how to guides on how to be better and live better by avoiding such relationships. You can reach out to counselors, life coaches, workshops, classes, and support groups.

4. **Take back your story** - In an emotionally abusive relationship, the abuser will force false narratives onto

the victim to justify their behavior. Which makes the abuser right, and the victim in a place where they feel they have no say about anything that happens through the relationship. The narcissist will often gaslight you in a way that alters your perception or reality about how you view the world and see yourself. This can cause long-lasting damaging effects on your mind, and on loving yourself because you have been told something false by someone you love.

Taking back your story is about undoing the abuser's lies and manipulations by being truthful with yourself. What you believe is the only thing that matters, or that should matter. As though this process can be difficult, it is possible and can be done only when you have successfully completed the stages of healing after the relationship is over.

How to Trust Others and Yourself Again

If you are in the process of leaving the narcissist, then you may be feeling pretty numb with devastation right about now. Life might seem so dark right now that you really don't know where to start picking up the pieces. The thing to try to remember in this state is where were you mentally before your encounter with the narcissist? You were probably confident, or more confident than you are now, believed in the good of others, You may have even been a little assertive with your own boundaries. You put these in place so that you wouldn't fall into an abusive relationship. Now that the relationship is over, part of what you feel may be just the fact that you can never trust someone else again due to the betrayal and hurt you went through. If you let yourself stay in this dark place, without opening your mind to the possibility that not all people are like that, then you will stay unpleasant and become bitter.

The new question is, how do you learn to trust again? Here are the steps.

1. Forgiveness

Through the abuse and trauma you may feel terribly stupid and beat yourself up a lot about how you could let yourself go through it all, You may be very negative one your self-image for not acknowledging the signs or staying longer. However, this can hurt your ego, and superego even more than what the narcissist put you through. The first step is to completely feel and take in every emotion you are going to undergo. Then be patient with yourself, time heals most wounds, but forgiveness is the strongest antidote. Instead of being your own worst nightmare, become your best friend, and really get to know yourself by forgiving yourself for the torture you suffered from. Take care of yourself through forgiveness and self-love, is one of the best ways you can get past such a difficult time.

When those negative thoughts of self-loathe pop into your mind, learn to acknowledge them, let them happen, and non-judgmentally watch them pass on. When they don't seem to go away, replace them with positive affirmations and mantras like "I got this." Also, the abuse was never your fault. The reason the abuse happened was that the narcissist is so insecure in his own skin that they attacked your weaknesses to make themselves feel powerful. There is nothing wrong with you, so forgive yourself for feeling this way too. Use this break-up as an opportunity to listen to your intuition more and grow more into who you are supposed to be, and who you want to be.

2. Listen to your gut (intuitive instincts)

Intuition is when your body gives you warning signs when something is wrong, or when you should be cautious before proceeding. Intuition can come in forms of racing thoughts right before you are about to do something, a feeling that you should run or freeze, or a vibe like chills or hairs standing up on your neck. Maybe a chill rush down your spine. Have you ever done something dangerous, or been in the line-up to a rollercoaster ride? That feeling you get as you step closer to the ride; your body and mind may be screaming at you not to go through with this. Or maybe your first kiss or date with someone you just met, that feeling you get right before your lips meet, or the feeling you have when you're sitting across a table from them on your date. This is your intuition. Sometimes your instincts scream at you to continue going, and other times, it tells you no. Learning to listen to it takes practice and life experience as you go through the roles of the ups and downs. Can you remember what you felt the minute you met your last girlfriend or boyfriend? The first impression is a judgment we make, usually right after our intuition speaks to us.

Has there been a time where you knew exactly what your insides were telling you, but you went against them anyways? Then what you feared would happen did? This is another form of intuition. So, when you think back to all the times you ignored your gut feeling about something, or someone, learn to listen to it next time.

3. Building new confidence

If you had confidence before your relationship, then it is likely that the narcissist has taken that away from you. The most daunting task in your recovery process is to build a new sense of confidence, different than you had before. This can only come as you build your self-esteem and your perception of who you are and who you want to be. So, maybe you didn't have a bunch of confidence back then either, which is why it is crucial to start building it now so that you can feel what you do deserve - worthy and appreciated from yourself. The good news is that by following the last two suggestion, forgiving yourself, and learning to listen to your intuition, you will be also building self- awareness, which promotes confidence. Your goals through these three steps bring your awareness levels to a place where you can look at how the narcissist hurt you, and which areas you need to work on the most. Which will tell you your strengths and weaknesses, and in the process of working through your weaknesses, with every one you overcome, your confidence level will go up as well.

This last stage in the process of building confidence cannot be completely done right unless you really look into the traumatic experiences you endured even before the narcissistic relationship. It could stem from childhood, and learn to break down, and walk through these barriers will help you see just how strong you really are, which will build a new level of confidence. Reaching out to support systems and teams like groups, classes, therapies, family, and friends, you will learn how to develop self-reflection. Self-reflection is crucial in learning more about yourself, and how you can see all the beautiful qualities the narcissist made you blind to. Take the pain that you feel, and use it to learn more about yourself, and you may just find out new things you never have seen about yourself before. By lighting up this whole new perception of yourself, you will find success and inner peace, which often leads to happiness.

Learning how to trust again is no easy task, but with patience and self-kindness, and the help of others, it is possible. By following the given steps, you will find that in time, you will develop authentic self-trust. When you have successfully learned how to reach inside yourself and trust who matters, then you can start putting your trust in new people who come into your life. This is because with the trust you feel inside yourself, you can trust that you know best when you are going to put your faith in someone else. This happens when you are perfectly in tune with your intuition. When you are in tune with your intuition, you will only follow your own gut instinct if you have the confidence to believe that you are right. And with forgiveness of your mistakes, you make along the way and patience to overcome whatever problems lie ahead for you, you will finally learn the true meaning of trust in yourself and in others.

CHAPTER 6

Ultimate Strategies to Overcome Narcissistic Abuse

You have made it this far, and may be wondering, so how exactly do I get past this devastation stage? How do I feel better? What are the exact things to do to get to a state where I have completely grown? There may be so many questions running through your head at this point. One of the first steps you can take is to cut off all ties, use the no contact rule - no matter what. Then it's all about self-care, and making a routine for yourself, like exercise which will greatly help you with the pain and stress you are feeling. Acts of kindness go hand in hand with self-awareness methods like how to be in the now with being mindful. Being mindful of your thoughts, feelings, and behavior can really help you to understand the behavior and feelings of others and has many more benefits. Then, there is EFT, Emotional Freedom Technique, which teaches us grounding methods, breathing techniques, mantra repeating, and other beneficial things you can do to make yourself feel better on those really tough days.

As briefly discussed in the previous chapters, EMDR Therapy is great for helping out with overcoming and pushing past feelings resulting from narcissistic abuse. And, while all of those are mainly to help your mental state, it is also good to work on your physical state with what you feed yourself, and what you can smell, opening up all your five senses. A diet plan, along with aromatherapy, can really speed the process when combined with the other mental methods.

No Contact

Perhaps, the first and most important thing to do when getting through a narcissist break up is to cut off ties completely. This means absolutely no contact - no matter what. Look at it as a no-contact order, except you are giving yourself this. Having no contact may hurt at first, but if you keep with it, it can really teach you things like self-respect, self-discipline, and will give you the much-needed space and time to do you for a while. As you got through the waves on devastation, some days may be harder, so it may be best to come up with a safety phrase when you are having trouble fighting the urge to reach out. Phrases like "he will just continue to hurt me if I reach out" or "What's the benefits of talking to them? It will do me no good, and I will be back where I started." You are so fragile at this point in time, so having no contact will give you both time to accept that it's really over, so you both can move on.

No contact may seem really difficult, or almost impossible, simply because they are all you know, you have lived your life with them whether they were a spouse, parent, or friend, and now it feels strange to live without them. You may be half in and half out about doing what you need to do to get better because you still have beliefs things could work. The mantra you need to repeat to yourself is, "narcissists won't change, because they can't unless they are willing to accept they are a narcissist." Which they won't because they don't see that there even is a problem. However, if no contact is not an option, there are other things you can do to avoid them. If you are co-parenting with them, then safety precautions need to be taken, and if they are a family member where you will see them at family events, you need to set serious boundaries.

What Exactly is No Contact?

There are some definite guidelines on the no contact thing and must be followed at all costs. When they contact you, for their hoovering methods, you need to really use skills you learn to ignore them at all costs. When you have urges to contact them, be mindful of them, and distract yourself by calling someone else or doing something else, and if those methods don't work, do an excellent workout to get you out of your head. Here are the guidelines:

- Block their number and all social media communication.

- Do not respond to any messages or emails that you receive.

- Not reading or responding to letters or cards. Fight the urge.

- Do not answer your door when they come over unexpectedly.

- Let your boss know that you are not available if they call you at work or show up at your work.

- Do not engage in external resources, like if they reach out to other people, you care about to get a rise out of you.

- Avoiding people who do not support your decisions and respect your boundaries about not talking about the narcissist.

How No Contact Supports and Promotes your Recovery

Healing is essential, and by following the no contact rule, you can finally gain a sense of peace (in time), with massive benefits to your mental health. Here is how;

1. Acceptance

Relationships can really shape your life regardless of if they are healthy or not. Every person in your life becomes a part of your experiences that you go through. Our experiences shape who we were, who we are today, and who is going to be or want to be. Every negative thing that you go through is an opportunity to implement positivity and engagement in self-growth. In healthy relationships, you are respected and honored without judgment.

When you get involved with a narcissist, quite the opposite happens. They make you become dependent on them, and take your strength from you, so that you feel trapped, or that you have to rely on you. This is their intention. Once this has taken place, and they have isolated you, and gotten you to a place of pure codependency, you feel as though you need them in your life. You feel as though even the abuse is hard, one day they will change if this, or if that. They won't then you are stuck in a vicious cycle living a nightmare. Acceptance is about accepting that the relationship is over, and you can gain this opportunity through no contact to do right for yourself.

a. **Letting all hope go** - The pattern that gets stuck on repeat from the narcissist is idolize, devalue, then discard. Without feeling any sense of empathy for you or your self-worth, the narcissist will cycle through this pattern indefinitely, leaving you feeling worthless. They put you on a pedestal and make you feel absolutely wonderful, then instantly drag you down, and discard your feelings by implementing blame. There is never a real conversation in between the arguments, and there are never real reasons they can give you to justify their behavior. This is never your fault. As long as you still hold what they need, or possess traits they can exploit, they will always hoover you or come back to poison you more.

The process of letting go of hope for them is that you can recognize this pattern, and reality should set in. If this sounds all too familiar, then all hope is lost for change, or "working things out." By holding onto this sense of hope, you are procrastinating your recovery, and sadly, it is false hope.

2. Addiction –

With acceptance, you must understand that you are not "in love," or "holding on" for a reason. You are simply addicted to the emotions that the narcissist makes you feel. How much time do you spend a day thinking about the narcissist? How do you feel when they punish you for it? Think about the silent treatments, for example. Do you feel pain when you think about how they treat you as opposed to how you treat them? Do you feel insane? or even physically ill?

These feelings you feel have now caused you to feel addicted to them. It's called trauma bonding in which they implement to keep you around. To keep you thinking about them. In the idolizing phase, they keep you 'high' on the highs of the relationship through their actions, once they know everything is okay, and you are hooked all over again, they shift into the devaluation phase. Which is the mental abuse stage where they tell you everything that's wrong with you and can even set you up to do what they want you to do, so that when you do it, they can devalue you even more. Then, to keep you from running away, they implement little doses of love through the torture. Which sets you up to stay addicted. To recover, **no contact at all** is best.

a. **Behavioral conditioning** - You crave the narc's attention and validation, and despite the abuse, you continue to chase the next high they give to you because it feels as though it outweighs all the bad. The narc then gives you your "hit," by hoovering you or baiting you back in through the first stage of idolization once again. This is done to you deliberately so that when they call, you are programmed to respond. If you don't respond, you feel as though you are in danger, or something seriously wrong could happen. This is how they form your actions to behave, think, and feel the way they want you to. It's also called a brainwashing technique.

By breaking this cycle through no contact, you can reprogram your own mind, and take control and power back from your abuser.

3. Heart, mind, and soul aid –

Behaviors are driven by what you think, and how you feel or manage your emotions. Narcissistic abuse represents cognitive dissonance and denial. Cognitive dissonance means that you have conflicting beliefs to what you originally believed. Which results in confusion, distress, and to get out of it, you are driven to fix the contradiction you feel. So, this is why trust is necessary so that you don't question your beliefs, and you are confident that they cannot be countered by a narcissist. From the confusion of everything you once believed to now being everything you are unsure of if you should believe causes you to live in survival mode. In which you may feel depressed, anxious, panic, restless, lack of trust, paranoia, fear, social isolations, obsessive or intrusive thoughts, anger, night terrors, or nightmares, and numbness.

Whatever you feel, you cannot start your healing process until you work through the pain and every emotion that comes with the pain. This cannot happen until there are no more ties between you and the narcissist. From the moment you implement no contact with your narcissist, you can start to embrace the positive healing measure that you must take to become healthy again. Just remember, when you grieve and become devastated, you have started healing. It may not feel like it, but it's better this way.

How Exercise can help you Heal from Narcissistic Abuse

Exercise can help with many disorders such as depression, anxiety, and mood disorders because the endorphins that rush through your body helps heal your body, mind, and soul. Exercise can also work to heal from abuse as well. Chronic abuse or narcissistic abuse shrinks the prefrontal cortex (front part of the brain) and medial temporal cortex (deep, center part of the brain). Anxiety results from long term stress, which includes problems with planning, decision-making, and socializing. When we undergo narcissistic abuse or bullying for a long period of time, our brain changes, which is not your fault or your control. The brain does this, to set up natural, and instinctive defense mechanisms against the abuse. When we exercise, it increases the thickness of our brain, which is essential for healing it.

However, every exercise has its own effect on the brain, and you must understand which exercises you do for proper brain structure and healing. It has to be a certain exercise designed, especially for healing the brain. Follow the next steps to start healing your brain with these specific exercises.

Step One - Choose an exercise from the list

- Brisk walking, jogging, or running

- Stepping stairs, or marching

- Bike riding

- Elliptical training.

The reasons these exercises are implemented strictly for brain development is because they are simple and repetitive. They all use patterns, which in order for your brain to grow, and heal, it is essential to have predictable measures be taken. This is because, with the emotional abuse that has happened, your life has been sporadic and unpredictable. Using high-stress exercises (anything that puts stress on your body), actually produces the cortisol chemicals to release, and can cause more anxiety at this very vulnerable state.

Step Two - Get started

Basically, you have to get the will or overpower the urge to sit around, and just start doing the exercise that you picked. If you feel uncomfortable and want to stop, fight that urge too. Exercise may be uncomfortable because, in the first two minutes of the exercise, your body is getting used to it, which means you might experience your heart rate increase, and your breath to quicken. This is a good sign because it means your brain is getting used to the idea of the pattern and predictable exercise.

Vow to yourself, you will do this every day for half an hour or more. After ten minutes into your workout, the 'feel good' chemicals will kick in, and your exercise will become easier. After ten minutes, with the endorphin surge, the prefrontal cortex (responsible for stress management) relaxes, which creates a controlled environment that your brain has been craving. Then you need to stay in this 'zone' for twenty minutes or more to get the best results. When you practice these exercises every day, you create a routine, which is also essential for brain healing from the abuse you implemented.

If you cannot go for twenty minutes at first, don't sit down, or relax, slow down, or just take a stepping break (where you step in one place), while focusing on your breathing. Go at your own pace, but keep it steady, and make challenges along the way. The goal of the exercise is to feel a sense of euphoria afterward because your brain is getting more oxygen and blood flow. This is a short-term effect that you can feel right away.

However, a long-term healing exercise for greater effects, and better releases of endorphins, you will need to practice this thirty-minute exercise for three to four weeks, about five times a week. The brain requires constant engagement and will not heal as you need it to after abuse has taken place if you don't commit to this.

Acts of Kindness

Acts of kindness mean that you do things for other people, for no reason, and having no expectation of getting it in return. Kindness is contagious in the very aspect that people who witnessed the act of kindness become inspired or motivated to want to do the same thing. This will make the chances of 'paying it forward' increase at a higher level. Then when you do something kind for someone else, you will also feel good, as it causes a feel-good emotion to stem right in the base of your brain. When you do kind things for other people in front of a group of people, you have just caused a domino effect, because they will feel inspired to do the same thing.

Here is a list of the massive benefits that acts of kindness associated with:

- **Increases the 'love' hormone** - Witnessing acts of kindness produces the oxytocin hormone (which is what you feel after or during a sexual act) This hormone lowers blood pressure and improves heart health. Oxytocin increases our self-esteem and confidence levels, as well.

- **Increases energy** - At the *"Greater Good Science Center,"* they did a study where they observed participants who helped others or acted generously to others. The participants reported feeling stronger, calmer, and less depressed. This also increases feelings of self-worth.

- **Increase in lifespan** - Volunteer work as a result of helping people for free tends to lower aches and pains. After sifting out contributing factors to health like exercise, gender, habits, marital status, etc. people 55 years of age and older who volunteered had a 44% increase in living longer.

Which is stronger than the effect of exercising daily and eating healthy your whole life.

- **Increases Pleasure** - Recent research implemented from *'Emory University,'* that when you help someone, your brain's reward centers light up, leaving you with what's called a 'helper's high.'

- **Increase in serotonin levels** - Serotonin is a chemical in your brain needed to promote feelings of balanced happiness. Low levels of serotonin are one of the reasons why people suffer from anxiety and depression. Kindness stimulates or activates this chemical and calms you down, heals you, and makes you happy.

- **Decrease in pain** - Endorphins are the brain's natural painkiller. When you help others, or 'pay it forward,' you produce more endorphins and get endorphin rushes. Also, endorphin rushes come from exercise as well.

- **Stress Decrease** - It is known that acts of kindness or generous people have 23% less cortisol running through their body. Cortisol is a stress hormone, and so when it is not being produced enough, you are a happier person.

- **A decrease in feelings of anxiety** - Anxiety sufferers accomplished helping others for six days a week. After one month, their moods increased, there was an increase in relationship satisfaction and a decrease in social isolation.

- **A decrease in blood pressure** - According to Dr. David R Hamilton, acts of kindness create emotional warmth, which releases the hormone oxytocin. Oxytocin released the chemical called nitric oxide, which dilates the blood vessels. The dilation of blood vessels reduces blood pressure, which makes sense that we can now look at oxytocin as a "cardioprotective" hormone.

What is EFT?

EFT stands for Emotional Freedom Techniques. EFT is used to help heal and recover from narcissistic abuse. This technique does not need to be guided by a professional therapist and can be done all on your own, wherever, and whenever you need.

EFT was founded by Gary Craig who was a Stanford trained engineer which he studied multiple acupressure techniques used for healing. The problem was that acupressure from what therapists used were complicated combinations of acupuncture points. So, Craig developed an easy formula called "tapping" on main acupressure/puncture points while concentrating on a problem. Using the system Craig found, happens to be considered effective for issues like anxiety, depression, abuse, phobias, and even PTSD or physical illnesses.

Five Ways EFT for Narcissistic Abuse Recovery Helps

1. **EFT helps reduce stress, depression, and anxiety** - In Traditional Chinese Medicine (TCM) negative feelings and emotions such as depression and anxiety are a result of blocked energy called "meridian" channels. The tapping in EFT forms and regulates new energy (chi) and removes emotional blockages.

2. **EFT helps lower cortisol levels (a stress hormone)** - After you get chi flowing from Craig's tapping technique, the newfound energy can reduce cortisol. Since cortisol put weight on the belly, and in the gut, it can also help you lose weight if you aren't developing so much.

3. **EFT helps decrease PTSD symptoms** - Panic attacks nightmares and phobias are very responsive to EFT treatment. However, do not rely solely on EFT for reducing these symptoms, as it takes therapy and exposure therapy methods to help cope with it. In severe cases with PTSD, consider seeing an EFT practitioner.

4. **EFT helps physical pain associated from narcissistic abuse** - Studies have proven to show that EFT helps extraordinarily with physical pain.

5. **EFT helps in healing childhood wounds or trauma.** - Narcissists look for people who have childhood wounds and trauma, so that they can exploit these symptoms and make matters worse. They do this because people that have childhood trauma are easy victims to get them to do whatever they want. EFT can build self-esteem, and by building your self-esteem, your old wounds will gradually recover and worked on.

Tips on Using EFT to Heal

You will need numerous sessions of EFT to heal from narcissistic abuse. There are layers to EFT, which is called "aspects." EFT can heal some problems, as shown above, instantly, for in-depth or deeper issues. You will need to undergo the "aspects" of EFT to fully or almost fully heal from narcissistic abuse. After tapping on one aspect, or layer using EFT, if you don't find it helpful, try a different layer or aspect until you find the right fit. For example, if you tapped on fear due to a car accident, and it only helped slightly, you would then focus on tapping on something more specific like feeling trapped. This way, you have hit a breakthrough into your true healing when implementing EFT.

What are Grounding Techniques?

Grounding techniques are a form of mindfulness to bring you back to the present moment. It is practiced for the purpose of training your brain to focus on what is here, and now instead of focusing and worrying about the past or future. In your case. Worrying about the past trauma, or the future about what the narcissist is going to do, now that it is over. Grounding is usually taught to you by a therapist and can be used to cope with and manage anxiety, depression, panic attacks, PTSD or C-PTSD, among other disorders.

Anxiety sufferers, or people who suffer from mood disorders, or abuse, and trauma, usually find themselves lying awake at night due to excessive, and uncontrolled thoughts. These thoughts worry about everything you could have or should have done in the past. Also, worrying about what is going to happen in the future. This is where grounding techniques come in. To bring you back to the present. Most grounding techniques focus on all five of your senses, touch, smell, sound, sight, and taste. However, there are no right or wrong methods to use when using grounding strategies. The following grounding techniques are the most beneficial for anxiety and trauma from recovering from narcissistic abuse.

1. **Concentrate on your breath** - You are intentionally, and without changing your breath, focusing solely on your breath. When you feel anxious or overwhelmed, your breath may be short and shallow, causing you to hyperventilate. You may not even notice it, and so when you intentionally bring your attention to your breath, focus on the rhythm of it. If it is short and shallow, gradually bring it back to normal. Like mindfulness breathing, the goal of grounding yourself when you are in a frenzied state, you take in a breath, count to ten, hold it for a couple of seconds, then release. At first, it may make you dizzy, but just make it a point to focus on your

breath and breathing patterns. It will center you and bring you back to this present moment.

2. **Physically hold something.** - Grab something such as a stuffed animal, a cup, a rock, or anything that you can see, feel, and use your senses with. Look at this item as if you were seeing it for the first time. For example, imagine you are caveman holding an eraser for the first time ever. What does it smell like, feel like, taste like, does it make a sound? What does it do? What color is it? What does it look like? Think about this item, where did it come from? How was it made? Being completely in this moment with the eraser, focus solely on the object you are holding.

3. **Repeat a mantra** - Think of a calm word, or phrase, and repeat this in your head until you feel calmer. It could be as simple as "toasty," or "warm." It could be as intricate as "I am okay, this is a false alarm," when having a panic attack. Or it could be as uplifting as "I got this, I am strong." Whatever mantra you choose, make sure it is either uplifting, simple, or makes you feel good.

4. **The 5,4,3,2,1 exercise** - This exercise brings you to the present moment by helping you focus on your surroundings. It gets you out of your head and back to what is happening now and around you. The great thing about this exercise is that you can do it anywhere at any time, and write it down, or just do it. The exercise includes:

    a. **Five** things you can see

    b. **Four** things you can feel

    c. **Three** things you can hear

    d. **Two** things you can smell

    e. **One** good thing about yourself

5. **Get up and do something physical** - So, imagine you are in a bubble about an arms width all around you. Whatever is upsetting you outside this bubble, may make you want to change scenery. When you feel flustered or upset, changing your surroundings may be the best until you feel better. You could go to the bathroom and run water on your hands. While focusing on the texture, or the way it feels on your skin. You could rub lotion on your hands, continuing to rub it in until there is no

more, counting how long it takes to disappear. Make a cup of tea, and focus on the warmth of the mug, the color of your mug and the taste of your tea. You could literally do anything and focus on absolutely everything you are doing.

The more grounding techniques you do, the easier it will be to continue to stay in the moment while you are doing things. If you practice this all the time, it will come to you as second nature, and you may even notice that you are completely present in everything you do. The grounding methods are strictly for those days where you are having a difficult time with flashbacks, or obsessive thoughts about your ex, or what could happen. When the what, the why and the how gets the best of you, think about a grounding technique and practice it.

What is EMDR Therapy?

EMDR (Eye Movement Desensitization and Reprocessing Therapy) is a type of therapy used in PTSD and C-PTSD recovery. It reduces the physiological distress accompanied by traumatic memories or flashbacks. This is when participants intentionally focus on their memories, while at the same time concentrating their attention outside themselves. It is a way to control your memories instead of them controlling you. For example, say you abused as a child, your therapist would ask you to close your eyes, go into a room in your mind, and play the memory. While asking you to take a deep breath, without you saying anything, they would guide you on how you control the memory. Some instructions they would say are pausing the memory, rewind the memory, change the color of the memory, fast forward. Then repeat.

If done successfully, you teach your brain that you are no longer back there, and you are an adult now looking at your memories in a third person type of view. They ask you how you feel about the memory, and then ask you how you feel now. Then gradually get you to feel different about your memory and perceive it differently so you can get relief from the power or control it has over you now.

Another example of this would be to have your eyes open but focus on your therapist's hand tapping, while also remembering what happened to you before. EMDR has been thoroughly studied[2] and has proven to be very effective for coping with or managing a series of traumatic events. It works well because the rapid eye movement allows neural networks in the brain to open up, allowing access to memories. These memories can be re-

---

[2] https://www.ncbi.nlm.nih.gov/pmc/articles/PMC3951033/

thought about and reprocessed about how we see these memories while being in a safe environment, as opposed to where the traumatic event took place. Then the memories become replaced by how you feel about it. Instead of being terrified, or panicky about it, you would then associate the memory with uplifting, powerful, and empowering thoughts and feelings, because you gain control back. When this happens successfully, the nightmares and anxiety attacks associated with the memories are then reversed, or not present.

How EMDR Can Help Someone Who Has Experienced Abuse

Someone who has experienced physical, emotional, mental, verbal, or sexual abuse may have many negative memories attached to their experiences. During an EMDR session, the person is asked to focus on the details of their trauma and abuse while also watching the therapist make some form of movement for several seconds or minutes. While this is happening, the therapist may generate or ask you to focus on positive affirmations or thoughts about how the memory or trauma feels.

The goal for the session is that the details of the memories fade, the experience may feel less traumatizing, and the emotional impact may decrease. For example, the abused may now see the abuser as someone who is ridiculous brought on by humor or pity, in which the memories suddenly don't feel as much of a big deal to think about or to get upset about anymore.

This happens because the brain is open to the experience and becomes unblocked in which the participant now thinks differently about their past experience. This teaches us control.

Can EMDR be helpful for Narcissistic Abuse?

Narcissists implement all types of abuse to get what they want, as discussed. It's basically the means of what most people think about when they hear the word abuse. However, narcissistic abuse is dangerous, and the recovery may not be healed in a few short sessions of EMDR because the damage that is done is worse than the damage that stems from normal abuse. Narcissists will add a layer of abuse on top of the "normal" abuse because they intentionally deceive you, brainwash you, repeat certain behaviors to trap you, and so forth. They mess with someone's core identity and make them believe something other than what they are supposed to or brought up believing.

You can never tell what a narcissist's true intentions are, whether they are telling the truth or not, who they really are, what their pasts were like, what they think about, basically everything you will question yourself about when it comes right down to who they are. When you ask questions, they may seem irritated, or allow you to know the minimum details. They lie not just to others and you, but mainly to themselves. The same methods or tactics used in cults, a narcissist will use to brainwash their partners or victims.

Most of it happens without actually causing "memories" to happen. And so, when the abuser tries to explain the wrong or think about the wrong that has happened, they can't. Mainly because the narcissist takes advantage of the cognitive dissonances that develop in you, and they do this by using intermittent reinforcement. It's the little things that they do over time that build up and build up into what feels traumatic, but when you think of something or try to think of one thing, it seems petty, or very minor. This is how they betray, and trick and trap your mind into staying because they haven't actually done anything wrong - in their opinion.

EMDR helps by focusing instead on the memories, but the feelings attached to the narcissist, and the therapist guides you through the many minor events that have happened. Then teaches you how to control or perceive the events, or feelings differently. You can diminish their devaluation through EMDR, which results in having more confidence and a stronger sense of self-esteem.

What are Positive Affirmations?

Positive affirmations are phrases or statements that challenge negative or unhelpful thoughts. Basically, you come up with something motivating, inspiring, or something that builds your self-esteem and you repeat it. Kind of like a mantra. These affirmations can be encouraging, motivational, or anything positive that boosts your confidence and promotes a positive change in your life. If you want to make a long-term change about the way you feel and think, positive affirmations are what you need to practice daily. Here are some of the main benefits of positive self-talk:

- Self-affirmations have been proven to decrease stress.

- Self-affirmations have been used in interventions which lead to physical behavior.

- They can make us dismiss, or become noticeable to harmful health messages, and responding with positive change rather than staying in the negative surroundings.

- Affirmations have been linked to academic achievement implemented by the students that feel "left out."

Positive Affirmations for Victims of Narcissistic Abuse

One sure fire way to recover from the mental and emotional abuse that the narcissist has distilled into you is positive self-affirmation. When you talk nicely and be kind to yourself every day, you will start to love yourself for who you are, which creates a reversal effect of what the narcissist has made you believe. This creates a strong mental state in which you become more resilient to hurt, blame, and harmful inflictions inflicted on you from this point forward. Tell yourself the following affirmations daily, and you will regain a sense of empowerment, and speed up your recovery process.

1. **I am healing gradually. One day at a time. One step at a time.** - Reminding yourself that you are healing not only decreases the pain but reminds yourself that you are stronger than you think and

will heal one day at a time. It gives you something to look forward to, so that one day you won't have to say this but can replace it with something else more positive.

2. **I am focusing on my future while leaving the past behind** - Almost always, you will think about the past events from what the narcissist made you think and believe. You may catch yourself thinking about your relationship with them, the good and the bad. By saying this to yourself, when you catch yourself in that moment, you may find that it will help you to stay on track and focus on what is to come.

3. **I am loved and will be loved. I deserve love, care, affection, and respect** - When you catch yourself belittling your own self, or questioning yourself worth, repeating this affirmation to yourself should bring you back to what you do deserve. When you practice on how to trust and let go of the fear of something bad happening, this affirmation will do wonders for you and your recovery.

4. **I am making myself a priority through self-care** - So, most victims of narcissistic abuse put their own needs aside for the goodness, or to help their relationship. Not realizing that the narcissist has tricked you, or trapped you into these patterns, sometimes you may catch yourself putting your thoughts, and beliefs aside for someone else even now. Practicing this affirmation will remind you that you are important, and you deserve to come first.

5. **I know and trust myself** - Gaslighting, a certain technique an abuser will have you go through can make you become untrustworthy of yourself, and the good in others. This is so that you become dependent on them and stay under their control. By telling yourself that you trust yourself, you can move forward, believing that you do trust and know yourself well enough to follow your instincts and live an abuse-free life.

6. **I have created strict boundaries that I am going to stick to** - When you separate from a narcissist, they will inevitably try to hoover you back in. This is why it is crucial to keep the no contact and set boundaries. By setting boundaries, and sticking

to them, you can block out their attempts at "winning" you back. Most of the time, the reason why a narcissist will come back into your life is because your boundaries are not strong enough to push them out. This affirmation will remind you that you have set these boundaries, making it easier to ignore their hoovering techniques.

7. **I have the support of the most important people in my life** - A lot of people have a hard time asking for help, but when you say this to yourself, it will be a positive reminder that when you need it, your support system will be there. Take a look at everyone you know and contact the closest bonds you have. Then, ask them for the much-needed support to help you get through this difficult devastation time.

What is Aromatherapy?

Aromatherapy is a healing treatment that comes in the form of oil, called "essential oils." The oils are extracted from plants to promote health and well-being. It has gained more recognition for the science of medicine and healing. Aromatherapy has been used for healing purposes for thousands of years, stemming back to ancient cultures in China, India, and Egypt, among many other places. The natural plant extract can calm in balms, resins, and oils, and are known to have positive physical and psychological benefits.

The following list is a list of products in which the aromatherapy works through your sense of smell or rubbing the oils into your skin.

- Diffusers

- Aromatic spritzers

- Inhalers

- Bathing Salts

- Body oils, creams, lotions, or topical applications.

- Facial steamers

- Hot and cold compresses

- Clay masks

There are over one hundred different types of oils, and each has specific benefits for specific problems. For example, when you are sick, you would diffuse eucalyptus oil, or when you are anxious, you will rub or infuse bergamot into your pores.

The benefits of aromatherapy are as follows:

- Pain management

- Increase in sleep, and the quality of sleep

- Stress reduction, irritation, and anxiety

- Joint pain

- Reduction in headaches and migraines

- Helps manage the pain from birth labor

- Fight illnesses and speeds recovery

- Helps with digestion

- Boosts immunity

Aromatherapy can help with narcissistic abuse recovery because some oils make you feel calmer, and more at ease with the complications in life. It helps by managing or helping you cope with your emotions.

The Most Popular Essential Oils for Healing

As mentioned earlier, narcissistic abuse can take massive negative effects on the brain. So, to release emotional trauma from the baggage of your previous relationship, you must stimulate the amygdala for proper healing. Our sense of smell is the only five senses that we have that are directly linked to our frontal lobe area in our brain. The frontal lobe controls our emotions, which greatly affects the limbic system. The limbic system, as mentioned, is responsible for controlling your emotions such as fear, anger, depression, and anxiety.

The following list provides you with information about the most important essential oils for healing your brain when you have undergone such a traumatic and abusive narcissistic relationship.

1. Basi

This essential oil is helpful for coping with feelings of anxiety, panic, and uneasiness. It promotes calmness, provides strength and peace in mind, and body. It may be helpful when it comes to addictions as well. Which is essential for helping you overcome the self-sabotaging thoughts or behaviors that were implemented from your narcissistic relationship.

2. Cedarwood

When you go through change or a sudden crisis, this oil is for those times when you become overwhelmed, or fearful of the sudden adjustments in your life. The events of change can leave you feeling trapped or isolated. Cedarwood implements the effect of leaving you to feel grounded and stable. Cedarwood may leave you feeling focused, happy, and hopeful.

3. Lavender

Lavender oil is very beneficial in helping you manage a number of emotions. It is proven to help with anxiety, depression, irritability, panic attacks, and stress reduction. Lavender enhances the beta waves inside the brain, which helps to calm your mind and make you feel more relaxed.

4. Inner Child

These oil releases stress from our mental, emotional, and physical bodies. This oil helps with PTSD, managing feelings of abandonment, rejection, and neglect. An inner child brings you peace, feelings of "in love," and acceptance to yourself, as well as feelings of shock, and grief.

5. Bergamot

Bergamot is a natural antidepressant. When we feel like we are unlovable, or when something is extremely wrong with us, bergamot is our friend when we cannot get out of our heads. It is the oil that helps us realize things about ourselves. We may feel self-love, self-acceptance while getting rid of self-judgment, and self-loathing. Bergamot releases feelings of fear, blame, the craving for approval, shame, and emotional pain.

6. Frankincense

This oil implement feelings of truth. It invites the individual to let go of negative energy or vibes and cleanses the spirit and soul. It promotes feelings of peace and enlightenment.

7. Hyssop

Hyssop enables clarity and helps you connect to yourself, encouraging well-being. Hyssop rids your body of the stressful, emotional uncleanliness, removing feelings of guilt, and fear.

8. Melissa - Lemon Balm

Lemon balm is an immune boosting essential oil used for emotional turmoil and combats stress and feelings of being overwhelmed. This is helpful for people who isolate themselves and shut down or withdraw from the world.

Through recovery from essential oils, no contact, EFT, EMDR, positive affirmations, exercise and grounding techniques which you will learn through being mindful, your process of healing will take less time than if you weren't to practice these strategies. Narcissists poison your mind, they make you believe different from your own beliefs, and they never feel as though they do anything wrong. They hurt you through gaslighting and become your worst nightmare even after your relationship ends because of the effect they have on your mind. The strategies in this chapter are sure to bring you back on track and help you go into the direction you need to go. It will help you to identify future narcissists and set you up for a healthier and positive relationship in your future.

CHAPTER 7

Indications That you are Recovering from Narcissistic Trauma and Abuse

With everything that we have learned so far, whether or not you have started your recovery from the abuse, you may be wondering if you have even taken steps forward. Sometimes, it can feel as though you have taken steps forward, but many steps back. With this frame of mind, you may feel motivated to strive for success, and less inspired if you don't feel any different than when you started. The truth is, with every step forward, practicing the many techniques and strategies in this book, you will be on the right path, even when it doesn't feel like it. You may question whether or not you have made any progress because you still may be thinking or wondering about your abuser. You may miss the moments you shared due to the cognitive dissonances the narcissist has implemented. This will cloud your vision and taking any more steps forward may feel like an impossible task.

So, the question is, how do you know where you are in the progress of your recovery? Pay attention to the following signs, as these signs are clear indications that you are recovering.

1. **You realize and understand that self-care is an everyday priority** - This first sign is that you have finally come to the acceptance that when you put yourself first, you are making steps forward. Self-care is perhaps the utmost importance in recovering from your past trauma and abuse. Self-care may include things like saying no more often, taking a nap when you feel overwhelmed or tired, eating healthier, exercising daily, creating boundaries, and making wiser decisions. You are done making excuses as to why you can't, or reasons why you should be back

together. Instead, you are so focused on putting yourself first, that you don't feel like you have time for anyone else's "drama."

2. **You do everything you have to, to protect your physical and mental well-being** - You notice the identity of a narcissist, and you realize that their feelings were never real. You understand the pain you went through, or are going through currently, and have vowed to not let it happen again. You do not allow yourself to respond to their hoovering techniques and understand that if you continue down this path, things will get better. You have come to terms with the fact that you will no longer tolerate or accept being around negative influences and going back into a narcissistic relationship. You have a new sense of peace and have set up boundaries to continue feeling happier than you were.

3. **You don't care about what your ex thinks.** - Remember the time where you were sitting there, after your separation, and you wondered if they were thinking about you, what they were doing, and how they were living their lives without you. Maybe you missed them and wondered if they missed you too. You are now in a place where you don't think about or

wonder those things because you are fulfilling your own dreams, desires, ambitions, etc. You no longer spend time thinking about their hold over you, or what they think, because you don't have the time or patience to.

4. **You are more focused on your own life than what your ex is doing with theirs.** - Because you know that if you go back to your ex, you will only be living with the repeated abuse that you experienced before, you no longer care to be engaged with them. You are at a state where you have worked really hard to get where you are now and realize that the most important thing is to take care of yourself.

5. **You come up with solutions, rather than focus on your problems.** - You have come to a realization that you have the power, and strength to change your circumstances. You have accepted that control, and power is in your hands, and not theirs. For every action, there is a reaction, and it's your choice how you decide to respond. If you get an email from your abuser, instead of having the urge to read it, you just delete it. When you get a text, you find it easy to ignore it. When you see them or run into them, there are no longer the "in love" feelings you once had.

6. **You see the past abuse as an opportunity, rather than a punishment like you once had.** - Regardless if your low self-esteem or unconfident behaviors were stemmed from your childhood, or not, you now realize that going through the relationship of a narcissist was an opportunity to overcome these weaknesses. You no longer look at your ex, or anyone else for approval, or appreciation. You have come to a state of mind where you are strong enough to walk away from anyone who makes you believe against your beliefs and devalue who you are. You have officially become your own best friend, instead of your worst enemy, and you are now clear about why you experienced the abuse and forgive yourself because where you are now is where you need to be.

WAIT!!!

READ THIS BEFORE GOING ANY FURTHER!

How would you like to get your next eBook **FREE** <u>and</u> get new books for **FREE** too before they are publicly released?

Join our Self Empowerment Team today and receive your next (and future) books for **FREE**! Signing up is easy and completely free!!

Check out this page for more info!

www.SelfEmpowermentTeam.com/SignUp

Thank you for reading my book...

Don't forget to leave an honest review...

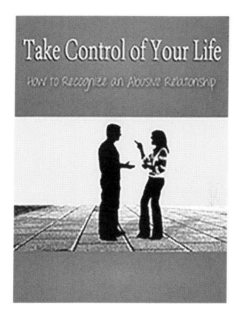

I'd like to offer you this amazing resource which my clients pay for. It is a report I written when I first began my journey.

Click on the picture above or navigate to the website below to join my exclusive email list. Upon joining, you will receive this incredible report on how to recognize an abusive relationship.

If you ask most people on the street what an abusive relationship is, chances are you'd get a description of physical abuse. And yes, that is most certainly an abusive relationship. However, abuse comes in many forms. The actual meaning of abuse is when someone exerts control over another person.

Find out more about recognizing an abusive relationship and learn how to take control over your life by clicking on the book above or by going to this link:

http://tinyurl.com/RecognizeAbusiveRelationship

CONCLUSION

N arcissistic abuse is perhaps one of the most extreme and damaging relationships you could ever experience due to the power they hold over you, and then the work you need to do to get better afterward. The main reason why people stay in narcissistic relationships is that they do not want to do the work to heal themselves. But, what they don't realize is that by staying in the relationship longer than they should, they will never have the opportunity to become a stronger, more peaceful self. The main reason you were a victim, is because you are self-conscious, and have questioned many things about yourself. It is so important to work on yourself now, during an abusive relationship, and years to come. Never stop working on yourself, to become the individual you were meant to be.

This book is the ultimate guide to help you get to where you have always been. So, take your trauma, and look at it as an opportunity to do something better for yourself. Be that strong, confident person you have always wanted to be. Do the work it takes to get the fulfillment you need. Fight the fear of change and ask yourself the important questions that will move you forward. Do I want to live in a bad relationship forever? What is the main benefit to me by allowing this behavior to happen? Who do I want to be? Everything you possibly imagined that you could have wanted is why you are in a narcissistic relationship. It is why you grabbed this book and read it to the end. Where you are in your life right now is exactly where you are supposed to be. The next step is what you choose. What kind of change will you make for yourself right now? What decisions will you make to make your future brighter?

The next steps may seem hard, but the decision is the easiest decision you will make. It should be simple. You want to make a difference in your life. You want to set a good example for your kids. You want to be the best version of yourself that you can be. You have a mountain to climb, but when you reach the top, it will have been the most worth fight you have ever done before.

So, what are you waiting for, make the next thing you do a step to a better future?

Cheers.

References

A Conscious Rethink – 12 Signs You're Dealing With a
   Malignant Narcissist (2018, June 07) Retrieved from
   https://www.aconsciousrethink.com/7145/malignant-
   narcissist/

A Conscious Rethink – 7 Healing Affirmations For
   Victims of Narcissistic Abuse (2019, February 26)
   Retrieved from
   https://www.aconsciousrethink.com/3949/7-healing-
   affirmations-victims-narcissistic-abuse/

Amygdala – The Brain Made Simple (2019, May 25)
   Retrieved from
   http://brainmadesimple.com/amygdala.html

Caroline Strawson – The Top Three Mistakes That Stop People From Healing From A Narcissistic Relationship (2018, June 10). Retrieved from https://www.carolinestrawson.com/the-top-three-mistakes-that-stop-people-healing-from-a-narcissistic-relationship/

Everyday Feminism – 5 ways to Rebuild and Love Yourself After An Emotionally Abusive Relationship (2018, July 27) Retrieved from https://everydayfeminism.com/2018/09/love-yourself-emotionally-abusive-relationship/

Fairy Tale Shadows – How EMDR Therapy Can Help with Narcissistic Abuse (2019, May 10) Retrieved from https://fairytaleshadows.com/how-emdr-therapy-help-with-narcissistic-abuse/

Good Therapy.org Therapy Blog – Common Questions Asked by People Healing from Narcissistic Abuse (2018, December 03) Retrieved from https://www.goodtherapy.org/blog/common-questions-asked-by-people-healing-from-narcissistic-abuse-0507184

Hack Spirit – Neuroscience reveals the shocking impact narcissistic abuse has on the brain (2019, May 19) Retrieved from https://hackspirit.com/3859-2/

References

Health Direct – Causes of Narcissistic Personality Disorder (NPD) (2019, May 23) Retrieved from https://www.healthdirect.gov.au/causes-of-npd

Healthline – What is Aromatherapy and How does It Help Me (n.d.) Retrieved from https://www.healthline.com/health/what-is-aromatherapy#side-effects

HelpGuide.org – Narcissistic Personality Disorder (201, March 21) Retrieved from https://www.helpguide.org/articles/mental-disorders/narcissistic-personality-disorder.htm/

Kim Saeed: Narcissistic Abuse Recovery Program – 6 Steps to Emotional Healing after Narcissistic Abuse (2018, January 05) Retrieved from https://kimsaeed.com/2014/08/27/6-steps-to-emotional-healing-after-narcissistic-abuse-1-is-most-important/

Kim Saeed: Narcissistic Abuse Recovery Program – The Top 8 Essential Oils for Emotional Healing (2018, January 03) Retrieved from https://kimsaeed.com/2016/03/21/the-top-8-essential-oils-for-emotional-healing/

Loner Wolf – 8 Signs You're the Victim of an Abusive Hoovering Narcissist (2019, April 29) Retrieved from https://lonerwolf.com/hoovering/

Mayo Clinic – Narcissistic personality disorder (2017, November 18) Retrieved from https://www.mayoclinic.org/diseases-conditions/narcissistic-personality-disorder/symptoms-causes/syc-20366662

Medical News Today – Hippocampus: Function, size, and problems (2017, December 07) Retrieved from https://www.medicalnewstoday.com/articles/313295.php

Mindbodygreen – When Forgiveness Isn't a Good Idea: A psychologist explains. (2018, March 12) Retrieved from https://www.mindbodygreen.com/articles/why-you-shouldnt-forgive-a-narcissist

Mindcology – 8 Types of Narcissists – Including One to Stay Away From at all Costs (2018, October 24) Retrieved from https://mindcology.com/narcissist/8-types-narcissists-including-one-stay-away-costs/

Narc Wise – Grounding Techniques for Panic attacks when Recovering from Narcissistic Abuse (2019, April 08) Retrieved from https://narcwise.com/2019/04/08/grounding-techniques-panic-attacks-narcissistic-abuse/

Narc Wise – How No Contact Supports Narcissistic Abuse Recovery (2019, January 27) Retrieved from https://narcwise.com/2018/04/02/no-contact-recovery-narcissistic-abuse/

Narcissism Recovery and Relationship Blog – 4 Key Stages of Healing After Narcissistic Abuse (2018, December 01) Retrieved from https://blog.melanietoniaevans.com/4-key-stages-of-healing-after-narcissistic-abuse/

Narcissism Recovery and Relationship Blog – Claiming Your Authentic Power After Narcissistic Abuse (2016, September 19) Retrieved from https://blog.melanietoniaevans.com/claiming-your-authentic-power-after-narcissistic-abuse/

One Love Foundation – 11 Reasons Why People in Abusive Relationships Can't Just Leave (2019, May 25) Retrieved from https://www.joinonelove.org/learn/why_leaving_abuse_is_hard/

Positive Psychology Program – Positive Daily Affirmations: Is There Science Behind It? (2019, March 05) Retrieved from https://positivepsychologyprogram.com/daily-affirmations/#science

Psych Central – 5 Emotional Freedom Technique Benefits in Narcissistic Abuse Recovery (2017, December 01) Retrieved from https://blogs.psychcentral.com/liberation/2017/12/5-emotional-freedom-technique-benefits-in-narcissistic-abuse-recovery/

Psychology Today – 3 Steps to Identifying a Narcissist (2019, May 23) Retrieved from https://www.psychologytoday.com/us/blog/5-types-people-who-can-ruin-your-life/201808/3-steps-identifying-narcissist

Psychology Today – 7 signs of a Covert Introvert Narcissist (2019, May 24) Retrieved from https://www.psychologytoday.com/us/blog/communication-success/201601/7-signs-covert-introvert-narcissist

Psychology Today – The Health Benefits of Tears (n.d.) Retrieved from https://www.psychologytoday.com/us/blog/emotional-freedom/201007/the-health-benefits-tears

Psychopath Free – Trust After Emotional Abuse (n.d.) Retrieved from https://www.psychopathfree.com/articles/trust-after-emotional-abuse.284/

Random Acts of Kindness – Make Kindness the Norm (n.d.) Retrieved from https://www.randomactsofkindness.org/the-science-of-kindness

Ravishly – 4 Stages Of Recovery From Narcissistic Abuse (2019, May 25) Retrieved from https://ravishly.com/4-stages-recovery-narcissistic-abuse

The Compatibility Code – The Compatibility Code (n.d.) Retrieved from https://www.compatibilitycode.com/book-resources/devastation/

The Minds Journal – 7 Signs You've Arrived as a Survivor of Narcissistic Abuse (2018, September 07) Retrieved from https://themindsjournal.com/7-signs-youve-arrived-as-a-survivor-of-narcissistic-abuse/

Verywell Mind – Are You Dealing With a Malignant Narcissist? (2018, November 08) Retrieved from https://www.verywellmind.com/how-to-recognize-a-narcissist-4164528

Wikipedia – Narcissistic Abuse (2019, May 13) Retrieved from https://en.wikipedia.org/wiki/Narcissistic_abuse

World of Psychology – How to Use Exercise to Overcome Abuse and Bullying and Heal you Brain (2018, July 08) Retrieved from https://psychcentral.com/blog/how-to-use-exercise-to-overcome-abuse-and-bullying-and-heal-your-brain/

YouTube – Getting Back in a Healthy Relationship After Narcissistic Abuse Pointer. (2018, August 18) Retrieved from: https://www.youtube.com/watch?v=kKxujjGMmm0

YouTube – Narcissist, Abuse Recovery: How Long Will It Take? (2017, March 30) retrieved from https://www.youtube.com/watch?v=mMxMsk-U1to

YouTube – Overcoming Loneliness After Narcissistic Abuse (2017, April 14) Retrieved from https://www.youtube.com/watch?v=jiDNJeUHG9c

YouTube - Reclaim Your Personal Power After Narcissistic Abuse – Codependents and Empaths. (2015, September 08) Retrieved from https://www.youtube.com/watch?v=bqmydqU-lqY

YouTube – The 5 Most Common Narcissistic Abuse Recovery Mistakes (2018, July 11). Retrieved from https://www.youtube.com/watch?v=cAOIdOKcFy8

YouTube – Why Can't I Stop Thinking About the Narcissist? (2017, September 13) Retrieved from https://www.youtube.com/watch?v=zxIzdXJ-eWg

Made in the USA
Columbia, SC
23 April 2020